Introduction

This book is simply a revised and updated version of the original "10
As with most things in life, attitudes, methods and approaches chan

When we were given the opportunity to reprint the book, we thought it would be a good ideal to add some new material to reflect our own change in thought.

Simplicity is often overlooked as a hindrance! Yet without mastering simply skills it is impossible to move training to a higher level. After many years of trying to be as imaginative and innovative as possible in our daily training routines we have found that the most effective drills are the basis ones. We have included several in the following pages.

Skills Drills simulate an aspect of the total game. They provide a controlled experience where players can develop new skills or refine the ones they've already mastered.

All coaches should attempt to use or design drills which are as closed to a game situation as possible. The more relevant the activity, the easier the players find it to transfer the learning to a game. It goes without saying that training sessions should be varied to maintain interest. With a little thought and pre-planning it should be possible for the coach to improve fitness levels and practice skills through the imaginative use of drills.

This book contains drills which have been collated over several years as well as many which we have devised or adapted ourselves. The drills for the most part can be used with players of all ages, simply by extending or contracting the distances shown. However, one should always bear in mind the experience of the players, the level at which they are playing and the relevance of the drill to their particular needs.

Although our main interest is Rugby Union, virtually all of the drills included are just as relevant to Rugby League. Indeed, even those which include skills peculiar to Rugby League, such as 'Play the Ball', can be adapted for use in the 15-a-side code.

We hope you enjoy the book and find it of use, but more so we hope it encourages you to devise your own drills for your own particular use.

Contents

Many of the drills in the book require more than one particular skill. To make them easier to categorise, we have placed them in the sections dependant on the main skill requirement. However, under each drill is the title 'Aims'. We have, where possible, listed all the attributes needed in each practice.

1

HANDLING SQUARE

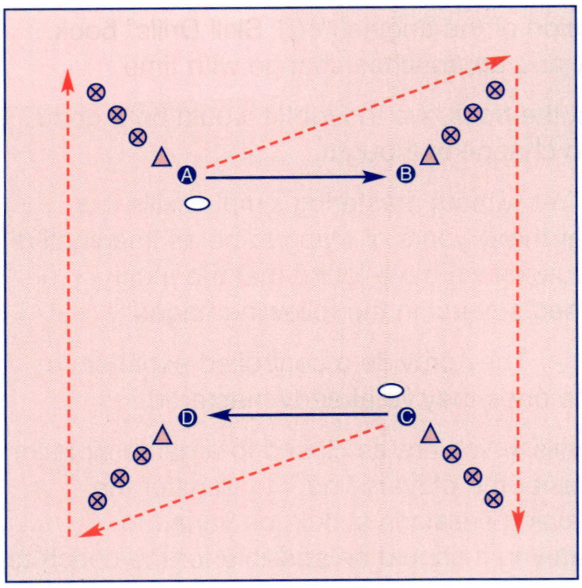

PLAYERS	4 Groups
EQUIPMENT	4 Markers and 2 Balls
AREA	10m x 10m grid
AIMS	Passing

	Ball
	Player
	Bag
	Shield
	Kick/Roll
	Run Without a Ball
	Pass
	Run With a Ball
	Cone/Marker

Explanation
Players in four groups at grid corners. Start with a ball at (A) and (C). (A) passes to (B), simultaneously (C) passes to (D). After passing, sprint around the outside of the other players, thus rejoining the drill at your opposite corner.

2

INSIDE BALL

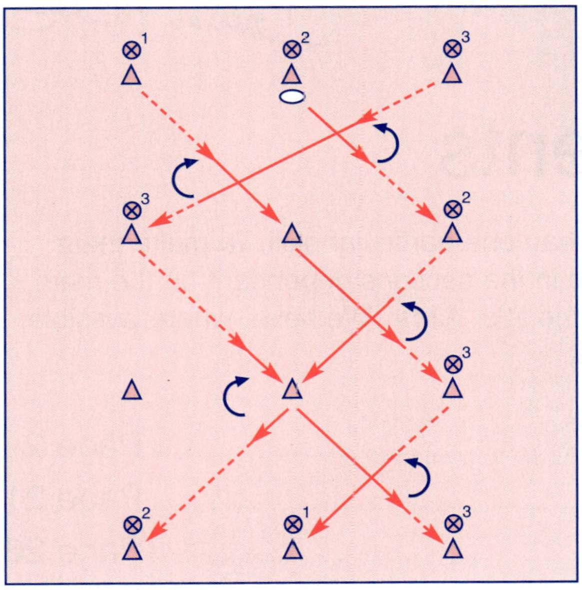

PLAYERS	Minimum 3
EQUIPMENT	1 Ball and 8 Markers
AREA	10m x 30m channel
AIMS	Passing, timing run, communication

	Ball
	Player
	Bag
	Shield
	Kick/Roll
	Run Without a Ball
	Pass
	Run With a Ball
	Cone/Marker

Explanation
Use groups of three players. Player (2) the ball carrier runs across and reverses to player (3). Player (3), who is now the ball carrier, runs across and reverses to Player (1). Player (1) then runs across and reverses to Player (2). The drill then continues in this manner.

3

SQUARE DRILL

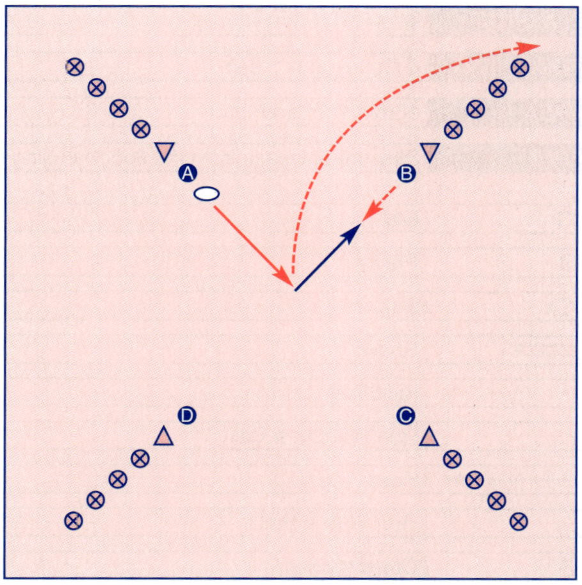

PLAYERS	Split group into 4
EQUIPMENT	4 Cones and 1 Ball
AREA	10m x 10m grid
AIMS	Passing, handling/timing the run

⬭	Ball
⊗	Player
◠	Bag
▬	Shield
–·–·–→	Kick/Roll
- - - - →	Run Without a Ball
——→	Pass
——→	Run With a Ball
△	Cone/Marker

Explanation
Four teams line up on grid corners. Begin the drill with a ball at (A). Player (A) runs to centre of the grid, stops and passes to player (B), who has just begun his run towards the centre. Player (A), after completing the pass, then fades away to line up behind the team he has passed to. The drill continues by Player (B) then passing to (C), etc. When the players are proficient and able to time their run, the ball should remain centralised throughout the drill.

4

HANDLING

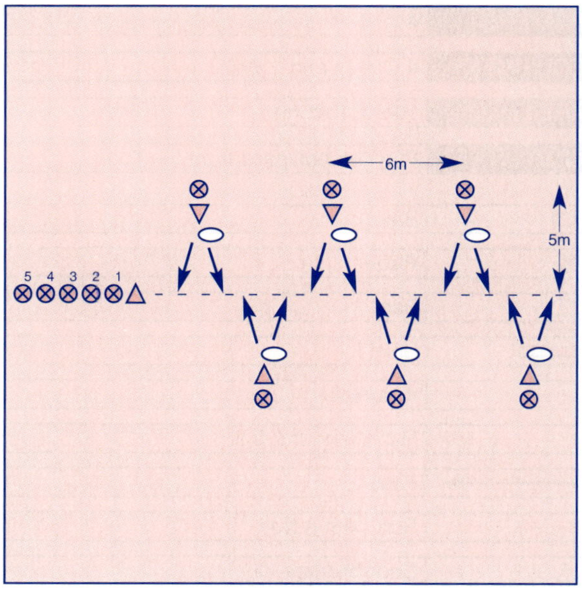

PLAYERS	15 Players
EQUIPMENT	10 Balls and 11 Markers
AREA	as in diagram
AIMS	Passing, handling, peripheral vision

⬭	Ball
⊗	Player
◠	Bag
▬	Shield
–·–·–→	Kick/Roll
- - - - →	Run Without a Ball
——→	Pass
——→	Run With a Ball
△	Cone/Marker

Explanation
Players (1) - (4) line up as shown. All other players stand next to a cone (5 metres from the mid line) with a ball facing the same direction as the runners. The attackers set off intermittently. As they receive an unexpected pass they must return it as quickly as possible to the original passer. Switch the players as required.

5

PLAY THE BALL

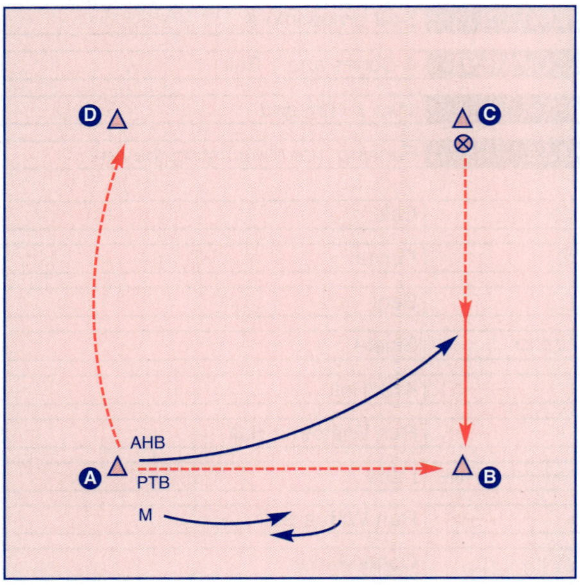

PLAYERS	4
EQUIPMENT	4 Cones and 1 Ball
AREA	10m x 10m grid
AIMS	Play the ball/pass from the floor/handling

⬭	Ball
⊗	Player
⌓	Bag
▭	Shield
-·-·-·→	Kick/Roll
---------→	Run Without a Ball
——→ (blue)	Pass
——→ (red)	Run With a Ball
△	Cone/Marker

Explanation
The drill begins with a 'play the ball' in corner "A". The acting half back passes to the runner coming from "C" corner, heading for corner "B" and follows. The marker also follows to oppose each 'play the ball'.
The player who started the drill by playing the ball, immediately retreats to corner "D" thus taking up the position of runner for the next 'play the ball'. The drill continues in this manner. Progress by introducing drop off passes or the acting half going alone and eventually mix up all permutations and rotate the players.

6

PLAY THE BALL

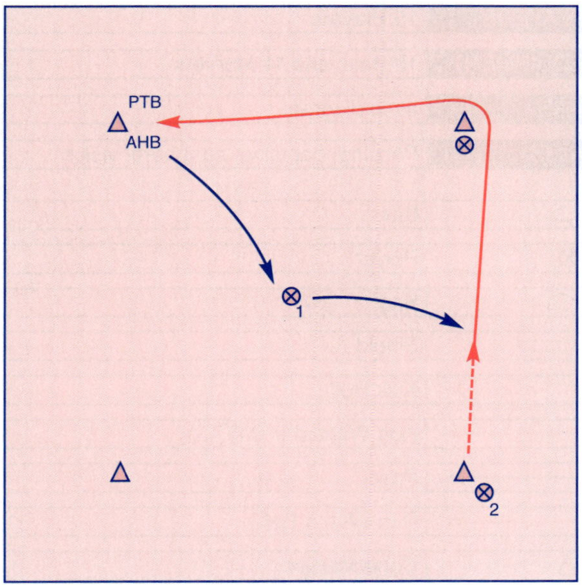

PLAYERS	4
EQUIPMENT	4 Cones and 1 Ball
AREA	10m x 10m grid
AIMS	Play the ball/pass from the floor

⬭	Ball
⊗	Player
⌓	Bag
▭	Shield
-·-·-·→	Kick/Roll
---------→	Run Without a Ball
——→ (blue)	Pass
——→ (red)	Run With a Ball
△	Cone/Marker

Explanation
The drill begins with a 'play the ball'. The dummy half passes to the first receiver (1) who in turn passes to the runner (2). The runner runs around the cone and into 'play the ball' position. Everyone else rotates one place, e.g.
P.T.B. becomes A.H.B.
A.H.B. becomes 1st pass (1)
1st pass becomes runner (2)

7

UNION JACK

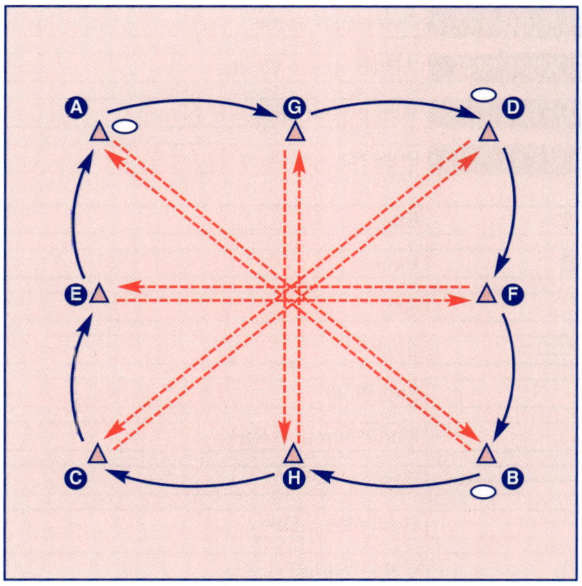

PLAYERS	8 players
EQUIPMENT	8 Cones and 2 Balls
AREA	15m x 15m grid
AIMS	Passing, handling, peripheral vision

⬭	Ball
⊗	Player
◠	Bag
▭	Shield
-·-·-→	Kick/Roll
- - - →	Run Without a Ball
——→	Pass
——→	Run With a Ball
△	Cone/Marker

Explanation

In a gridded area 15 metres x15 metres (smaller for children), Players (A) and (B) start with a ball each. On the word "Go", the balls are passed to the left. Each person having caught the ball, passes then runs across the grid, interchanging positions with their partners.

Partners = (A) + (B), (C) + (D), (E) + (F), (G) + (H)

8

TAG BALL

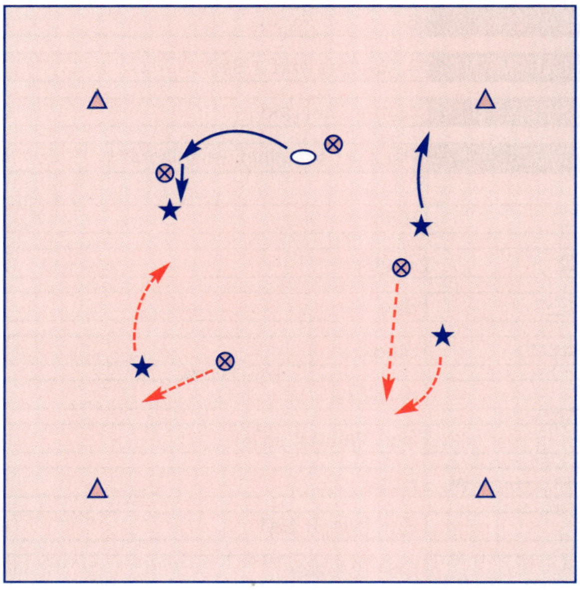

PLAYERS	Two equal teams
EQUIPMENT	4 Cones, 1 Ball and Bibs
AREA	10m x 10m grid
AIMS	Passing, handling, agility, communication

⬭	Ball
⊗	Player (Attacker)
★	Player (Defender)
▭	Shield
-·-·-→	Kick/Roll
- - - →	Run Without a Ball
——→	Pass
——→	Run With a Ball
△	Cone/Marker

Explanation

Divide the players into two equals, e.g. 3 v 3, 4 v 4. One of the teams in possession, attempts to touch the ball on the other group, without dropping it. The player in possession cannot run. Other players in the group must move around into a better position to receive a pass and effect a 'touch' on the opposition.

When a player is tagged he must the leave the area.

The game is contested against the clock with the second team attempting to better the first group's times.

9

HANDLING/MOBILITY

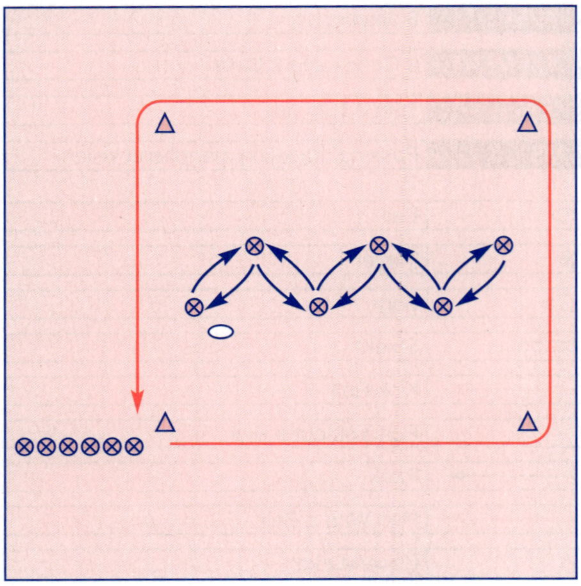

PLAYERS	Two equal teams
EQUIPMENT	2 Balls and 4 Cones
AREA	10m x 10m grid
AIMS	Passing, handling

	Ball
	Player
	Bag
	Shield
	Kick/Roll
	Run Without a Ball
	Pass
	Run With a Ball
	Cone/Marker

Explanation
Divide your players into two teams, set them out in a 10 metre x 10 metre gridded area (as per diagram).
One group carrying a ball, run around the perimeter of the grid one at a time, etc.
The other group, zig-zag pass, counting each pass they make, whilst the other team is running with the ball.
The roles are reversed, the team having made the greatest number of passes being the winner.

10

HANDLING

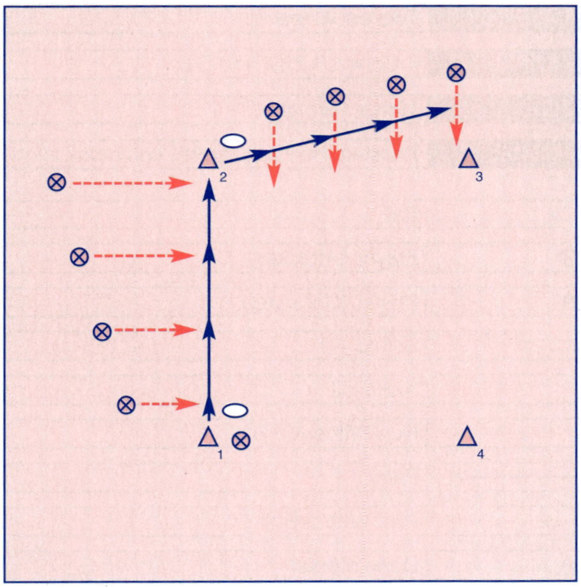

PLAYERS	5
EQUIPMENT	4 Markers and 1 Ball
AREA	15m x 15m grid
AIMS	Passing, handling, conditioning

	Ball
	Player
	Bag
	Shield
	Kick/Roll
	Run Without a Ball
	Pass
	Run With a Ball
	Cone/Marker

Explanation
Set up the area as shown the diagram, up to five players line out, from cone (1).
On the word "Go" the ball is passed along the line, with the final player receiving and touching down on the inside of cone (2). The other players, after passing, must loop round in order to re-align 'on' cone (2) (as shown in the diagram).
Otherwise the drill continues on cones (3) and (4) with player (1) restarting the play each time - rotate player positions.

11

FAST HANDS

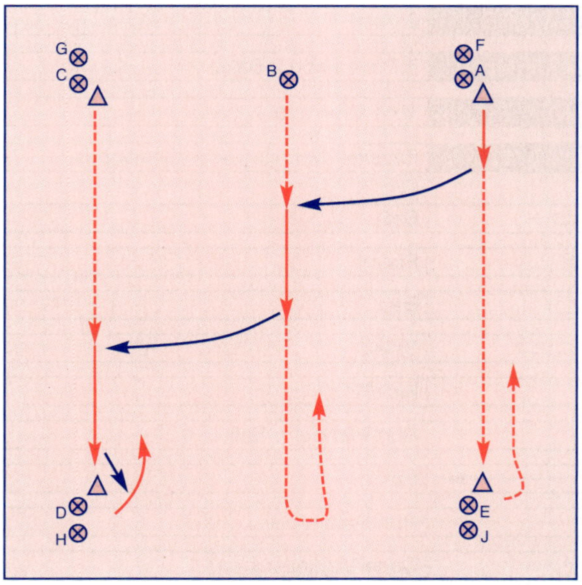

PLAYERS	Minimum 9
EQUIPMENT	4 Cones and 1 Ball
AREA	10m x 20m grid
AIMS	Passing, handling, conditioning

	Ball
⊗	Player
	Bag
	Shield
	Kick/Roll
	Run Without a Ball
	Pass
	Run With a Ball
△	Cone/Marker

Explanation

While running across the grid, player (A) passes to (B) and then onto (C). Having crossed the grid (C) turns the ball over to (D). (B) turns quickly to link the next set of passes (D) to (B) to (E). Once across the grid (E) turns the the ball over to (F). (B) having again turned quickly, links the passes from (F) to (B) to (G), as they return across the grid. Player (G) passes to (H) and the drill continues until (B) has turn ten shuttles.
Players rotate until all have linked the line as did player (B).

12

SQUARE DRILL

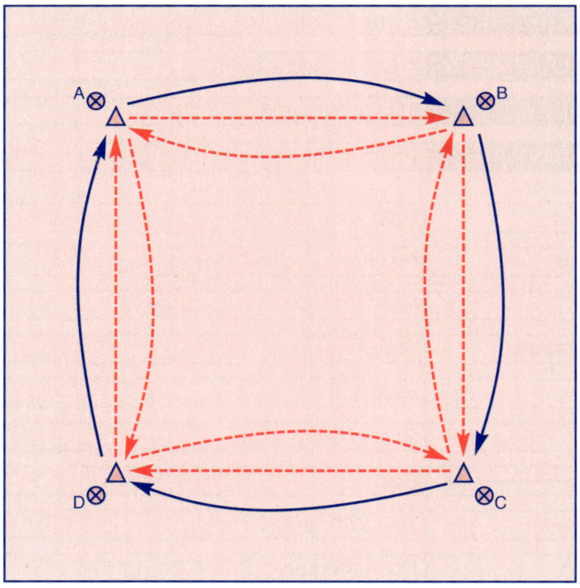

PLAYERS	4
EQUIPMENT	1 Ball and 4 Cones
AREA	5m x 5m grid
AIMS	Passing, handling, conditioning

	Ball
⊗	Player
	Bag
	Shield
	Kick/Roll
	Run Without a Ball
	Pass
	Run With a Ball
△	Cone/Marker

Explanation

The ball is passed around a five metre grid (A) to (B), (B) to (C) and (C) to (D). Immediately after passing, each passer follows and touches the ground at the foot of the receiver before returning to his original position to receive his next pass and continue the drill.

13

HANDLING FILE DRILL

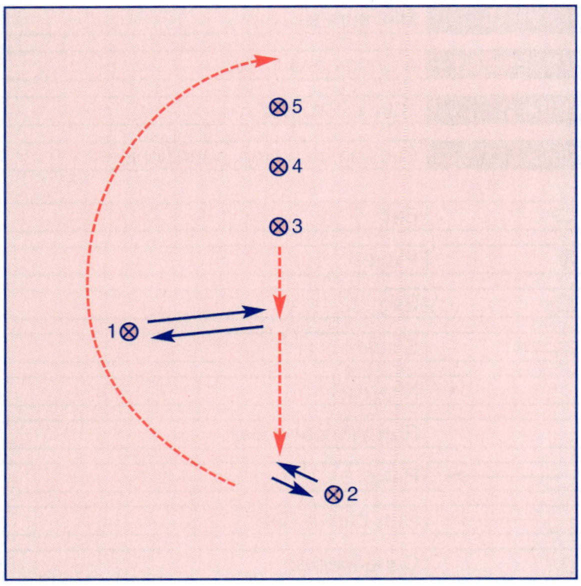

PLAYERS	6 (min)
EQUIPMENT	3 Cones and 2 Balls
AREA	10m x 7m grid
AIMS	Passing, handling and conditioner

⬭	Ball
⊗	Player
◠	Bag
▭	Shield
–·–·–·→	Kick/Roll
---------→	Run Without a Ball
——→	Pass
——→	Run With a Ball
△	Cone/Marker

Explanation

X1 & X2 stand in staggered formation in front of file. X3 runs between them. Takes a pass from X1 & returns it then takes a pass from X2 & returns it. X3 returns to back of line. X4 then begins. Change X1 & X2 every minute. Runners time their run.

Extensions:

(A) Pass at varying heights
(B) Pass off the ground
(C) Alternate sides that X2 &3 X3 pass from
(D) Reduce distance between X1 & X2

14

HANDLING FILE DRILL

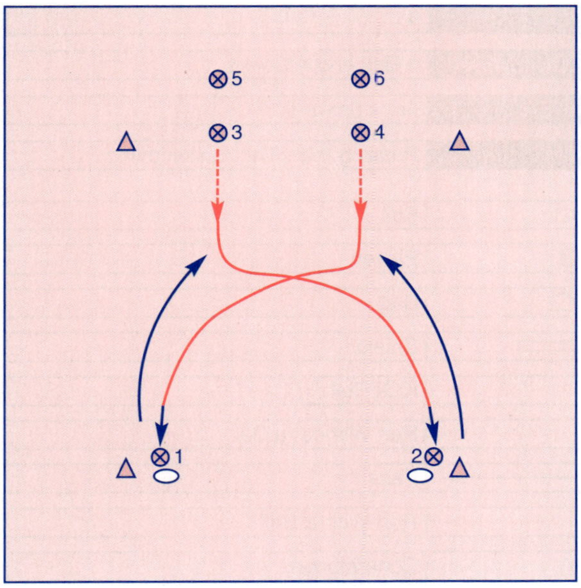

PLAYERS	6 (minimum)
EQUIPMENT	4 Cones and 2 Balls
AREA	10m x 10m grid
AIMS	Passing, handling and conditioner

⬭	Ball
⊗	Player
◠	Bag
▭	Shield
–·–·–·→	Kick/Roll
---------→	Run Without a Ball
——→	Pass
——→	Run With a Ball
△	Cone/Marker

Explanation

X1 & X2 stationary at end of grid. X3 & X4 move out together. X1 passes to X3. X3 cuts & scissors with X4. X4 returns ball to X1. X5 & X6 moves out. X2 passes to X6 who cuts & scissors with X5. X5 passes to X2. Drill continues. EMPHASISE CHANGE OF ANGLE & EASY "POP" PASS.

PROGRESSION: As X3 & X4 move out X1 may pass to either of them. Receiver cuts & scissors.

15

SQUARE DRILL

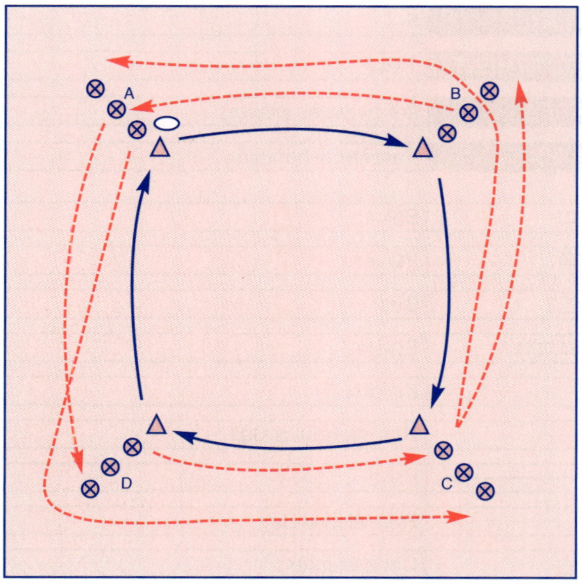

PLAYERS	4 Groups (maximum)
EQUIPMENT	4 Markers and 2 Balls
AREA	15m x 15m grid
AIMS	Passing, handling, conditioning

Ball
Player
Bag
Shield
Kick/Roll
Run Without a Ball
Pass
Run With a Ball
Cone/Marker

Explanation
Three or more players in each corner. The drill begins with (A) passing to (B) at the same time as (C) passes to (D). Immediately after passing, players run anti-clockwise to rejoin the drill at their opposite corner (see diagram). The drill then continues by (B) passing clockwise to (C's) corner and commuting anti-clockwise to corner (D). Likewise (D) passes to (A's) corner before commuting to corner (B).

16

FAST HANDS DRILL

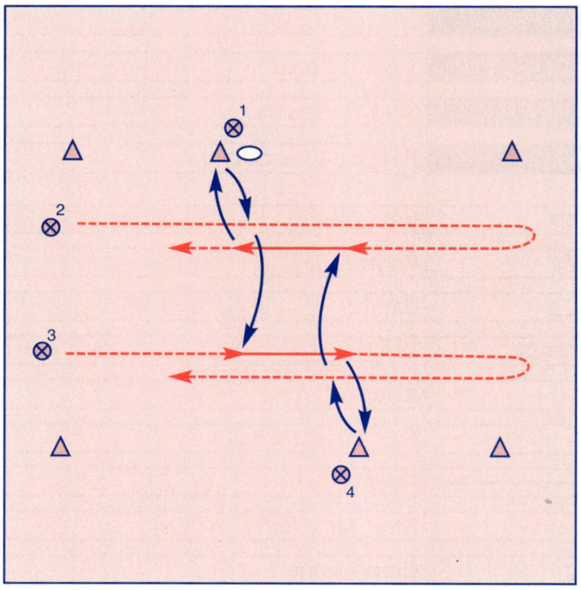

PLAYERS	Minimum 4
EQUIPMENT	6 Cones and 1 Ball
AREA	20m x 20m grid
AIMS	Passing, handling, communication

Ball
Player
Bag
Shield
Kick/Roll
Run Without a Ball
Pass
Run With a Ball
Cone/Marker

Explanation
The ball starts with player (1) on the outside of the grid. As player (2) runs past he is fed a short pass from, (1). Player (2) immediately releases the ball to player (3) in support. Player (3) then passes on to (4) positioned on the outside of the grid. On the return run (3) is fed a short pass from (4) and immediately passes on to (2) who returns the ball to (1).

Continue the drill and then alternate the players.

17

REACTION CATCHING

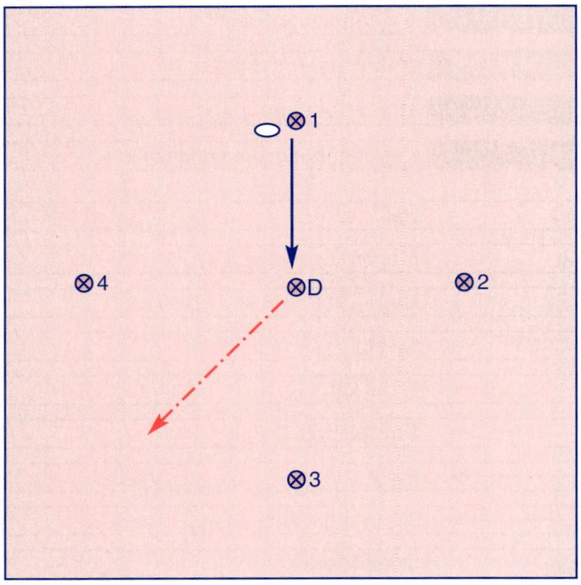

PLAYERS	5
EQUIPMENT	1 Ball
AREA	2m between players
AIMS	Passing & handling

⬭	Ball
⊗	Player
◠	Bag
▭	Shield
-·-·-·→	Kick/Roll
----------→	Run Without a Ball
——→	Pass
——→	Run With a Ball
△	Cone/Marker

Explanation
Four players surround central players (D). All remain stationary. X1 begins with the ball. X1 passes to D who flicks (taps) it in any direction. Nearest player must dive/jump etc to collect the ball. Whoever collects the tap or flick then passes to D who repeats the exercise. Central player is rotated every 30/45 sec.

Extension Change distances between players.

18

REACTION DRILL

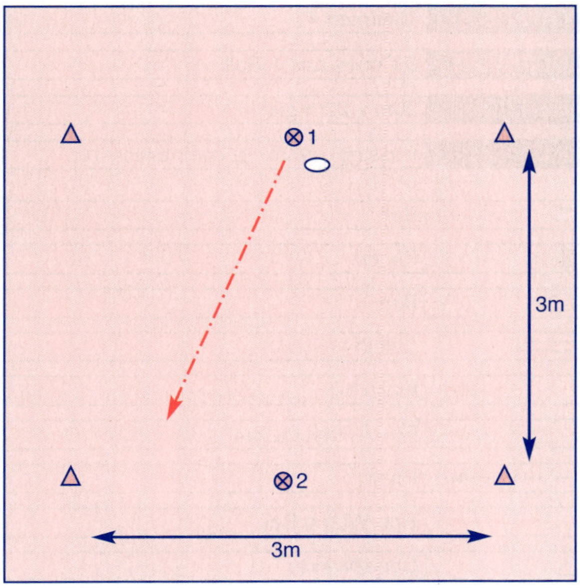

PLAYERS	2
EQUIPMENT	1 Ball 4 Cones
AREA	3m x 3m square
AIMS	Passing & handling

⬭	Ball
⊗	Player
◠	Bag
▭	Shield
-·-·-·→	Kick/Roll
----------→	Run Without a Ball
——→	Pass
——→	Run With a Ball
△	Cone/Marker

Explanation
X1 with a ball attempts to kick ball between markers (grubber type kicks, below waist height). X2 attempts clean pick-up/catch. Immediately passes back to X1. Change role after 1 minute.

19

CORNER POINT PASSING

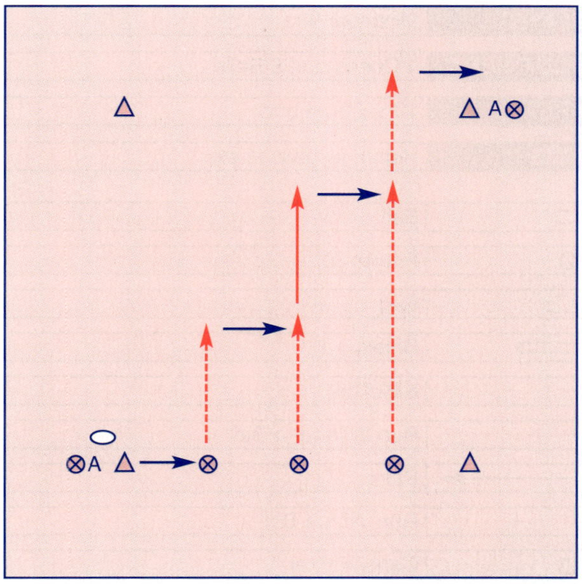

PLAYERS	5
EQUIPMENT	1 Ball 4 Cones
AREA	10m x 10m grid
AIMS	Passing & handling

⬭	Ball
⊗	Player
◠	Bag
▭	Shield
-·-·-·→	Kick/Roll
------→	Run Without a Ball
——→	Pass
——→	Run With a Ball
△	Cone/Marker

Explanation
2 players (A) stand on opposite corners. The (A) players do not move only receive & pass. The 3 X players pass in a short chain movement up and down the grid. Change A's after 45 secs.

Extension
Intro face passes etc.
Into (A) players on each corner to allow for scissors.

20

INSIDE/ONSIDE PASS GAME

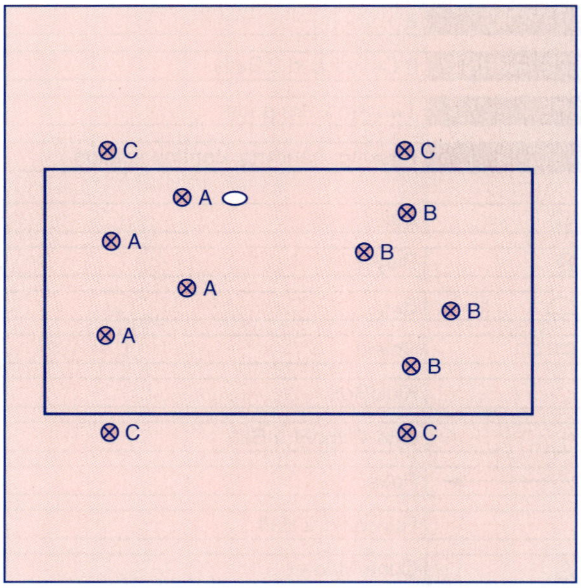

PLAYERS	12
EQUIPMENT	4 Cones 1 Ball
AREA	15 x 30 square
AIMS	Passing, agility and conditioning

⬭	Ball
⊗	Player
◠	Bag
▭	Shield
-·-·-·→	Kick/Roll
------→	Run Without a Ball
——→	Pass
——→	Run With a Ball
△	Cone/Marker

Explanation
All passes within the grid must be onside (backwards) passes except any to the outside men (C's).
However all passes from (C) which bring the ball back into the grid must be onside (Backwards passes), (C's) always play for the team in possession.

Rules Two handed touch means a turnover, lose possession (dropped ball, bad pass etc) mean a turnover.
Team gaining possession always attacked furthest goal-line. Games last 3 minutes then alternate teams.

21

QUICK HANDS DRILL

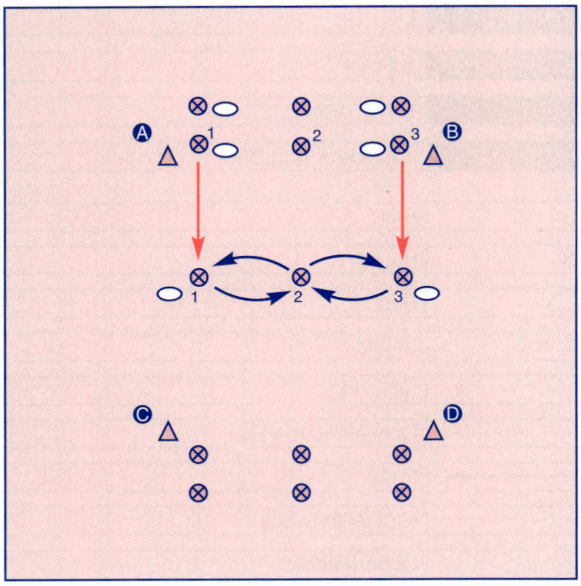

PLAYERS	Minimum 9
EQUIPMENT	4 Cones and 6 Balls
AREA	10m x 30m grid
AIMS	High/Low passes etc.

- Ball
- Player
- Bag
- Shield
- Kick/Roll
- Run Without a Ball
- Pass
- Run With a Ball
- Cone/Marker

Explanation
The group is split into 3's. The first 3 jog down the grid with the 2 outside players holding a ball. Player (1) will pass to player (2) who will immediately return the pass. As soon as player (2) has passed back to player (1), player (3) will pass his ball to player (2) who will immediately pass it back to him. This continues down the grid. On reaching the end, the next group take over and return back down the grid. The drill continues with the middle player rotating on a regular basis.

22

HANDLING DRILL

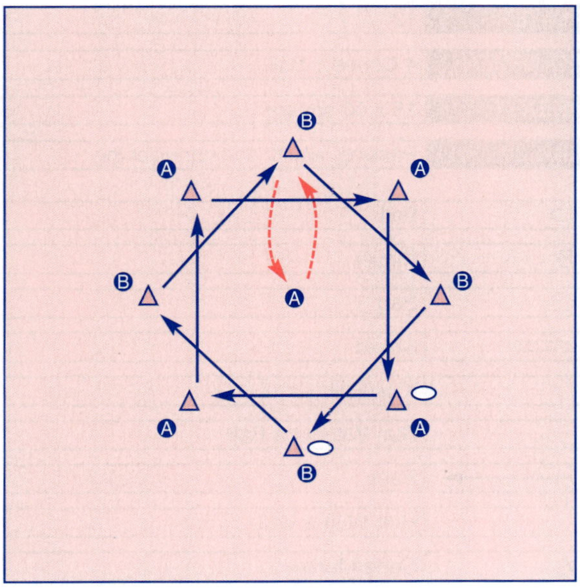

PLAYERS	8
EQUIPMENT	9 Cones and 2 Balls
AREA	Two 8m x 8m grids
AIMS	Passing, handling, communication

- Ball
- Player
- Bag
- Shield
- Kick/Roll
- Run Without a Ball
- Pass
- Run With a Ball
- Cone/Marker

Explanation
4 players are placed on the corners of an 8m grid (team A). They begin to pass the ball around the grid. Team B are also placed on 8m grid but this is placed in a diamond shape (as in the diagram). Team B also have a ball and begin to pass it it around their grid. After 1 minute the coach should blow a whistle or give a command. On this signal after a player has passed the ball they must run forward and touch the central cone, before back pedalling into place to receive another pass. After two minutes swap the teams and the direction of pass.

23

FAST HANDS

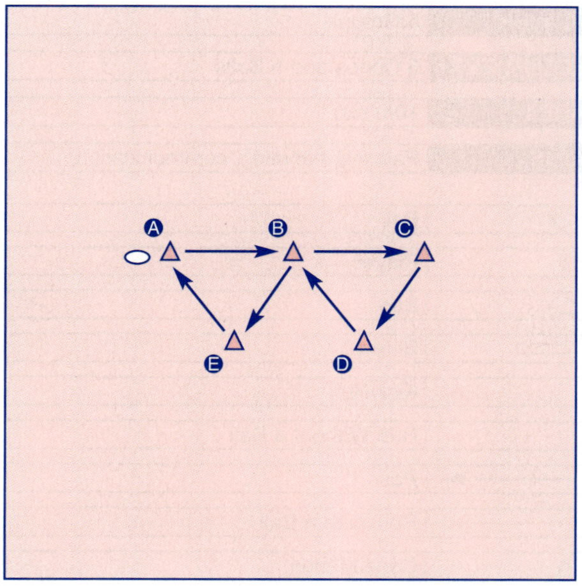

PLAYERS	5
EQUIPMENT	5 Cones and 2 Balls
AREA	W formation, 2m apart
AIMS	Passing, handling, communication

	Ball
	Player
	Bag
	Shield
	Kick/Roll
	Run Without a Ball
	Pass
	Run With a Ball
	Cone/Marker

Explanation
5 players are placed 2m apart in a 'W' formation. (A) begins with the ball. He passes to (B) who passes to (C) who passes to (D). (D) then passes to (B) who passes to (E) and finally back to (A). This continues for 1 minute. After a minute a 2nd ball is introduced for the final minute. Rearrange the group so all players are placed in position B.

24

INSIDE/SWIVEL PASS

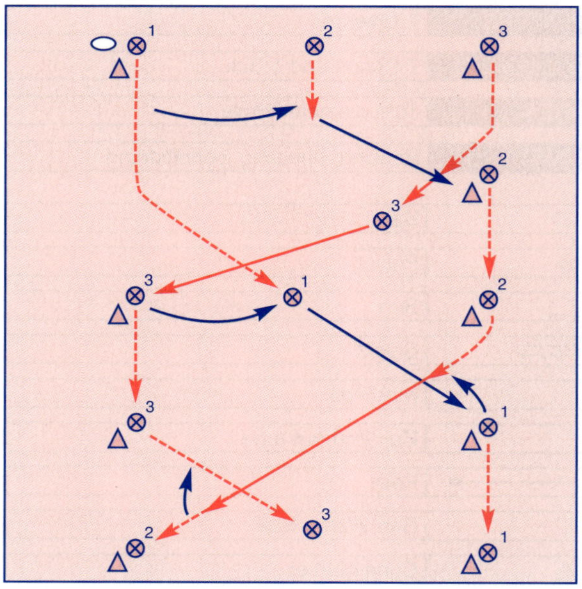

PLAYERS	3
EQUIPMENT	1 Ball and 10 Cones
AREA	50m x 10m corridor
AIMS	Passing, handling, communication

	Ball
	Player
	Bag
	Shield
	Kick/Roll
	Run Without a Ball
	Pass
	Run With a Ball
	Cone/Marker

Explanation
3 players line up at the top of the grid. Player (1) begins with the ball. He passes to player (2) and continues down the grid. Player (2) arcs across player (3) and executes a drop off pass to him. Player (3) now angles across the grid to player (1) who comes inside to the middle. Player (3) gives an orthodox pass to player (1) who then arcs across player (2) and executes a drop off and so the drill continues down the corridor.

25

STAR RUNNING

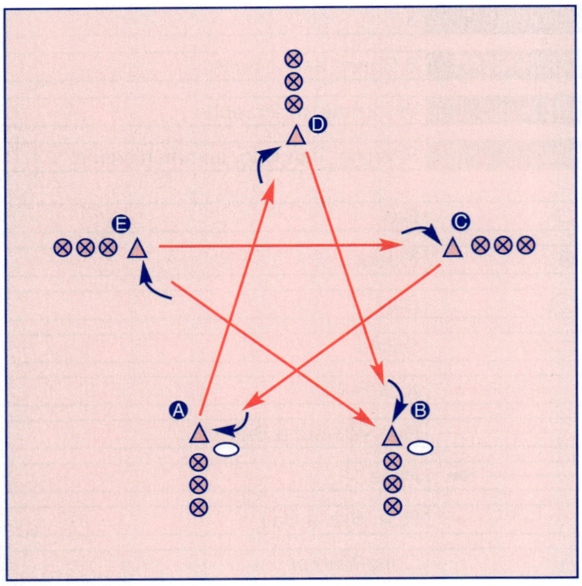

PLAYERS	5 Groups
EQUIPMENT	5 Cones and 5 Balls
AREA	10m star
AIMS	Passing, handling, communication

⬭	Ball
⊗	Player
⌓	Bag
▭	Shield
−·−·−▶	Kick/Roll
- - - -▶	Run Without a Ball
——▶	Pass
——▶	Run With a Ball
△	Cone/Marker

Explanation
Split the group into 5 stations – star shaped. Group (A) and (B) begin with a ball. First player from Team (A) runs to team (D) and pops up the pass to the first player. He runs to team (B) and so on. At the same time the first player in team (B) begins by running to (E). So that two balls are continuously moving. As the drill progresses add a ball to each station so that 5 balls are eventually in play.

26

HANDLING

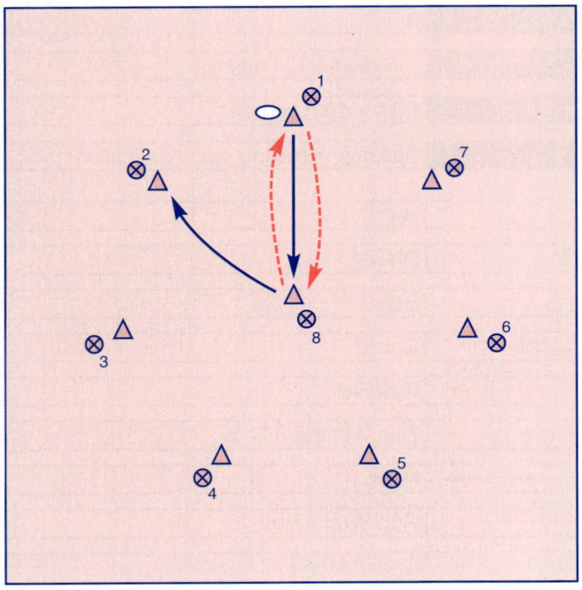

PLAYERS	7 Upwards
EQUIPMENT	7 Cones and 1 Ball
AREA	10m diameter circle
AIMS	Passing, handling, conditioning

⬭	Ball
⊗	Player
⌓	Bag
▭	Shield
−·−·−▶	Kick/Roll
- - - -▶	Run Without a Ball
——▶	Pass
——▶	Run With a Ball
△	Cone/Marker

Explanation
Players line up in a circle with one player in the middle. Player (1) passes to player (8) and follows the pass into the middle. Player (8) then passes to player (2) and runs to player (1)'s position. Player (2) passes to player (1) (who is now in the middle). Player (1) now passes to player (3) and runs to player (2)'s position and so on. (Give players exercises to do when not involved).

27

HANDLING DRILL

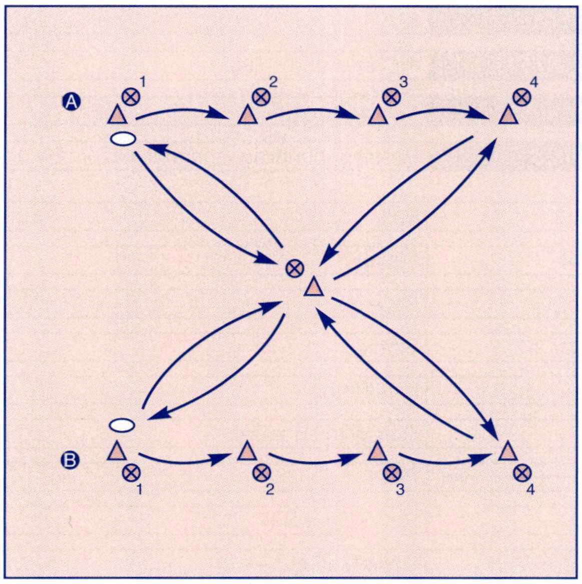

PLAYERS	9
EQUIPMENT	2 Balls and 9 Cones
AREA	10m x 10m grid
AIMS	Passing, handling, peripheral vision

⬭	Ball
⊗	Player
◠	Bag
▭	Shield
−·−·−·➔	Kick/Roll
- - - - - ➔	Run Without a Ball
——➔	Pass
——➔	Run With a Ball
△	Cone/Marker

Explanation

Player (1) in row A passes the ball to the man in the middle, who passes it back to him. Player (1) then passes to (2) who passes to (3) who passes to (4). He then passes the ball to the man in the middle who passes it straight back. Then player (4) passes to player (3) who passes to (2) and (2) to (1). The process then starts again.
Row (B) does exactly the same thing at the same time, however player (1) in row B doesn't pass to the player in the middle until he's passed back to player (1) in row A.
Rotate – the man in the middle after 2 minutes.

28

PASSING DRILL

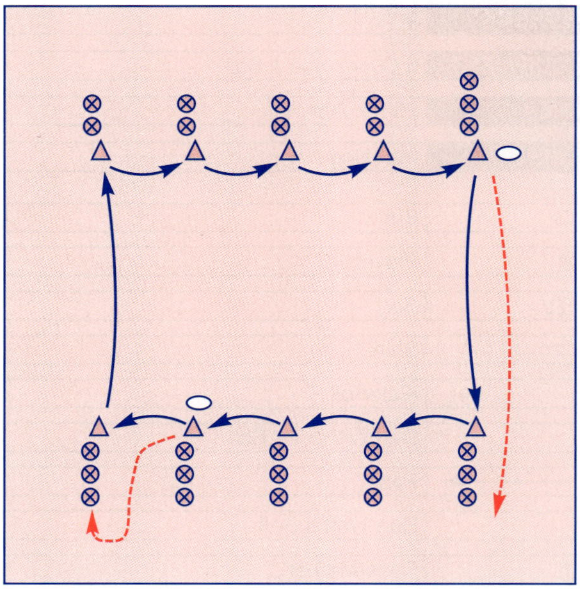

PLAYERS	Split the group into 10 teams
EQUIPMENT	10 Cones and at least 2 Balls
AREA	20m x 35m grid
AIMS	Passing, handling, decision making

⬭	Ball
⊗	Player
◠	Bag
▭	Shield
−·−·−·➔	Kick/Roll
- - - - - ➔	Run Without a Ball
——➔	Pass
——➔	Run With a Ball
△	Cone/Marker

Explanation

Spread the group evenly around the 10 marker cones. Begin with 2 balls at different places.
The player with the ball passes to the player at the front of the team on his left. As soon as a player has passed the ball he sprints to the back of the team to his left. More balls can be added dependant on ability.
After the players are competent change direction of the passes. Then get the players to pass to their left but sprint to the back of the team on their right and vice-versa.

29

CONTINUOUS ATTACK

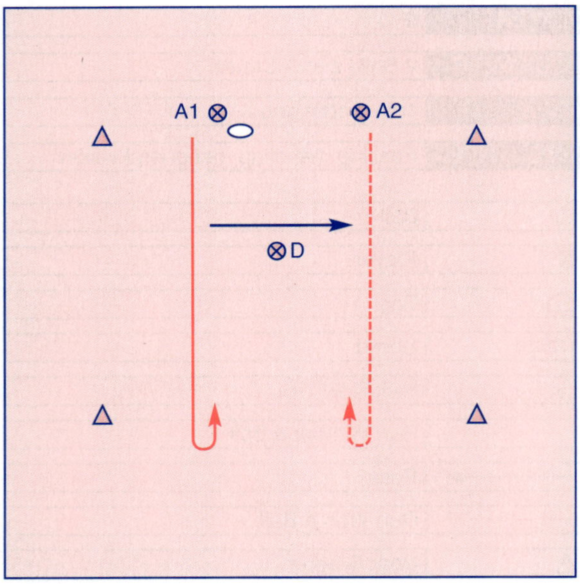

PLAYERS	3
EQUIPMENT	4 Cones and 1 Ball
AREA	12m x 7m grid
AIMS	Passing, handling, communication 2 V 1

⬭	Ball
⊗	Player
◠	Bag
▭	Shield
-·-·-→	Kick/Roll
- - - - →	Run Without a Ball
——→	Pass
——→	Run With a Ball
△	Cone/Marker

Explanation
3 Players per grid, A1 & A2 attack continuously 10 times, D is the defender, Aim is to score 10 out of 10. Change defender after each set of 10.

30

CONTINUOUS ATTACK

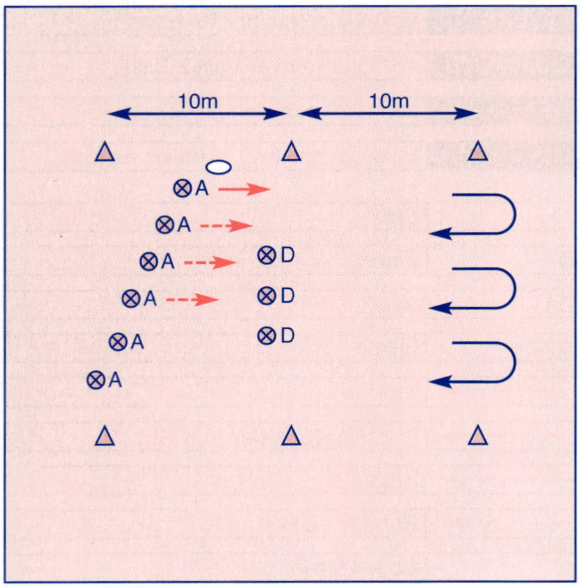

PLAYERS	9
EQUIPMENT	6 Cones and 1 Ball
AREA	25m x 20m
AIMS	Handling

⬭	Ball
⊗	Player
◠	Bag
▭	Shield
-·-·-→	Kick/Roll
- - - - →	Run Without a Ball
——→	Pass
——→	Run With a Ball
△	Cone/Marker

Explanation
Defenders (D) can only move side to side, Attackers (A) attack each end alternately, Attackers have 10 attempts, Change defenders after set of 10.

Emphasise:
- Drawing defence.
- Holding up the slide.

31

SQUARE DRILL

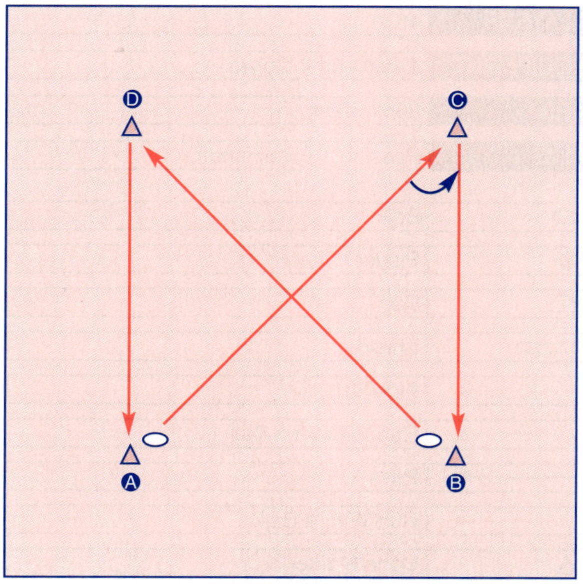

PLAYERS	4 Groups
EQUIPMENT	4 Cones and 2 Balls
AREA	10m x 10m
AIMS	Passing, handling

	Ball
	Player
	Bag
	Shield
	Kick/Roll
	Run Without a Ball
	Pass
	Run With a Ball
	Cone/Marker

Explanation

4 files line up on each corner. A ball is given to the front man at (A) and (B). They begin the drill by running diagonally to the opposition corner and passing to the front man. This player then runs down the side of the square (i.e: (A) passes to (C) who runs straight towards (B). Players running from (A) and (B) always run diagonal and players running from (D) and (C) always run straight. The drill is continuous.

Extension: Add more balls.

32

MULTI SKILL DRILL

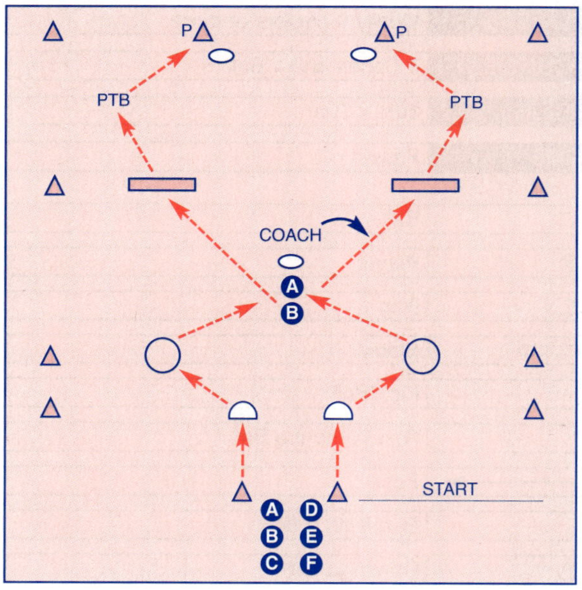

PLAYERS	At least 18
EQUIPMENT	2 Shields, 2 Bags, 2 Tubes, 2 Balls, 12 Cones
AREA	20m x 20m channel
AIMS	Multi Skills Work

	Ball
	Player
	Bag
	Shield
	Kick/Roll
	Run Without a Ball
	Pass
	Run With a Ball
	Cone/Marker

Explanation

The first pair of players (A & B) run forward and hit the bags 5m in front of them. They regain their feet quickly and peel left and right (as though chasing) from marker to hit through the oncoming tubes. They regain their feet to form up as double markers in front of the coach. When they are formed up, the coach will point either left or right. This will indicate which direction the front marker will chase off to and hit the shield at the side. The second marker will hold before moving off to hit the shield. After driving back the shields they run towards the two players on the end line who roll out a ball toward each of them. The players must regain possession safely and regain their feet to quickly face the start line and deliver a quick play the ball, before jogging back to the start. After 3 minutes change the players around.

33

LINE PASSING

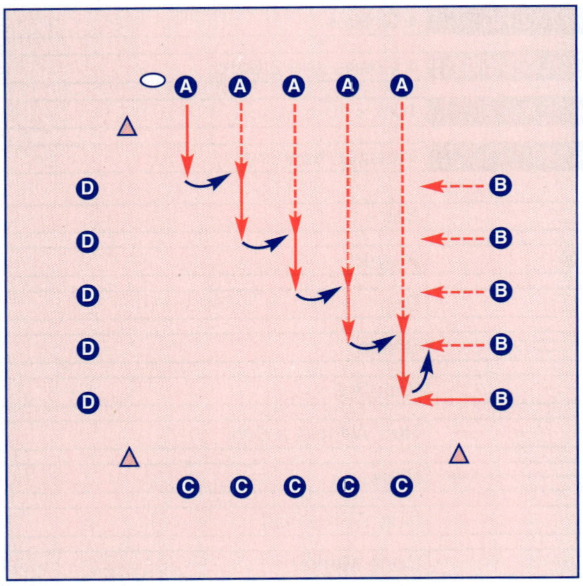

PLAYERS	4 Groups
EQUIPMENT	1 Ball and 4 Cones
AREA	20m x 20m
AIMS	Passing – Fast Hands

	Ball
	Player
	Bag
	Shield
	Kick/Roll
	Run Without a Ball
	Pass
	Run With a Ball
	Cone/Marker

Explanation
(A) line moves forward passing the ball. When end man received, he hands on to the first man in (B) line. (B) line moves forward across the grid and the end man passes to (D). (D) triggers off line (C) and the drill continues.

34

SQUARE DRILL

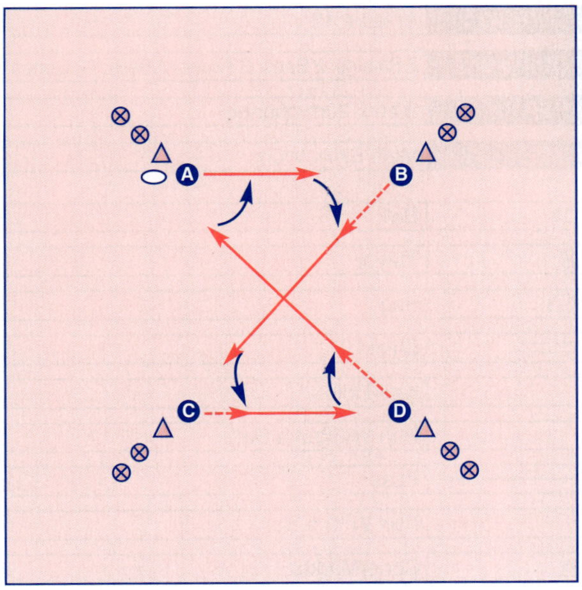

PLAYERS	Ideally 8 players or more
EQUIPMENT	4 Cones and 1 Ball
AREA	10m x 10m
AIMS	Passing

	Ball
	Player
	Bag
	Shield
	Kick/Roll
	Run Without a Ball
	Pass
	Run With a Ball
	Cone/Marker

Explanation
A passes to B (on the run)
B passes to C (on the run)
C ~~A~~ passes to D (on the run)
D passes to A (on the run)
And so on .....

35

DROP OFF & PASS SQUARE

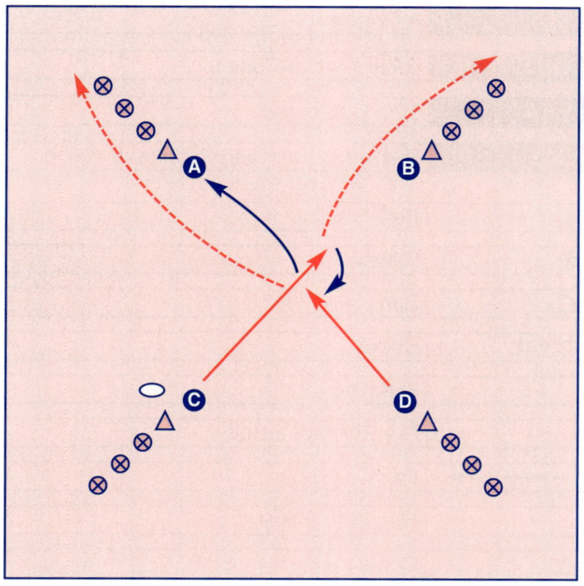

PLAYERS	4 Groups
EQUIPMENT	4 Cones and 1 Ball
AREA	15m x 15m
AIMS	Passing, communication, timing

⬭	Ball
⊗	Player
⌓	Bag
▭	Shield
-·-·-·→	Kick/Roll
- - - - →	Run Without a Ball
→ (blue)	Pass
→ (red)	Run With a Ball
△	Cone/Marker

Explanation
(C) runs towards (B) – (D) runs towards (A). In the middle (C) executes a Drop-off pass to (D) and (D) immediately delivers a long ball to (A). The drill then continues in the same manner with (A) dropping off (B), etc.

36

HANDLING SQUARE

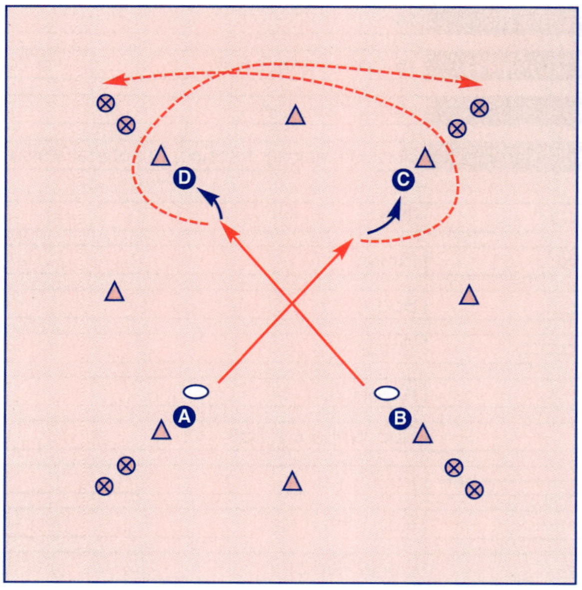

PLAYERS	4 Groups
EQUIPMENT	8 Cones and 2 Balls
AREA	10m x 10m grid
AIMS	Peripheral Vision – Conditioner

⬭	Ball
⊗	Player
⌓	Bag
▭	Shield
-·-·-·→	Kick/Roll
- - - - →	Run Without a Ball
→ (blue)	Pass
→ (red)	Run With a Ball
△	Cone/Marker

Explanation
(A) and (B) begin with ball, run diagonally and pop-up pass and rotate to the left, i.e. (A) will run and pass to (C) then join the back of (D), (B) will run and pass to (D) and join back of (C).
Extension: Introduce more balls.

37

SQUARE DRILL

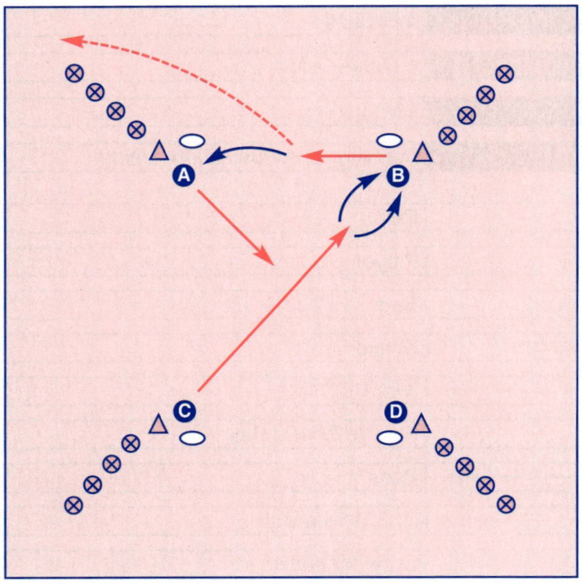

PLAYERS	4 Groups
EQUIPMENT	4 Balls and 4 Cones
AREA	10m x 10m grid
AIMS	Passing & Handling/Peripheral Vision

⬭	Ball
⊗	Player
⌓	Bag
▭	Shield
-·-·-›	Kick/Roll
- - - -›	Run Without a Ball
——›	Pass
——›	Run With a Ball
△	Cone/Marker

Explanation
Each player with a ball, at the front of each file, runs towards the cone diagonally opposite and lays off a pass to the player at the cone, and takes a pass back before turning left and passing to the man at the next cone along. e.g: (C) runs toward (B) and passes, received back, turns and runs towards (A) before passing to the man at the front of (A) file who repeats the same procedure.

38

REACTION DRILL

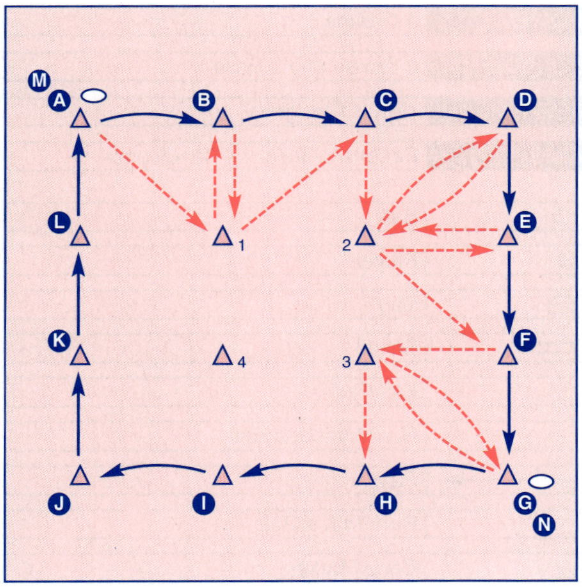

PLAYERS	14
EQUIPMENT	16 Cones and 2 Balls
AREA	15m x 15m grid
AIMS	Decision Making, Passing, Peripheral Vision

⬭	Ball
⊗	Player
⌓	Bag
▭	Shield
-·-·-›	Kick/Roll
- - - -›	Run Without a Ball
——›	Pass
——›	Run With a Ball
△	Cone/Marker

Explanation
12 players are spaced equally around the grid. Two balls are placed at diagonally opposite corners with (A) & (G). An extra player is placed at each of these corners. On command the balls are passed to the left around the grid. Player (A), after passing, will run forward to marker (1) in the centre and then return to slide to the next one along. (B), on receiving and passing the ball, will run out to cone (1) and then slide left to the next cone along. (C) will receive and pass the ball and run onto cone (2), before returning and sliding to the next cone along.
NB: This only works when passing to the left.

39

DECISION MAKING 1

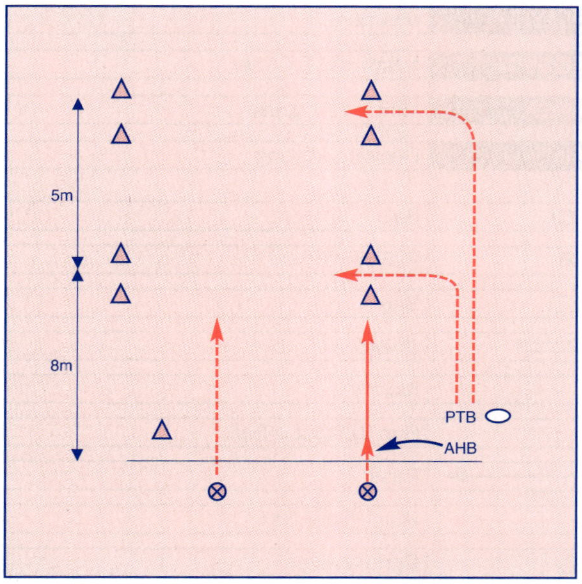

PLAYERS	Minimum 4
EQUIPMENT	10 Cones and 1 Ball
AREA	10m x 30m channel
AIMS	Decision Making, Support

⬭	Ball
⊗	Player
◠	Bag
▭	Shield
-·-·-·→	Kick/Roll
- - - - →	Run Without a Ball
——→	Pass
——→	Run With a Ball
△	Cone/Marker

Explanation

Four players per group. Two in a ball play situation and two attackers (1) and (2). The drill begins when the dummy half passes to player (1) who starts out with support up the channel. The player who played the ball enters the channel at the 8m mark, defending in a 2 v 1 situation. Likewise the acting half back enters at the 15m mark, posing another 2 v 1 situation for attacker (2).

NB: When beaten, the defender does not chase back. Rotate players.

40

DECISION MAKING 2

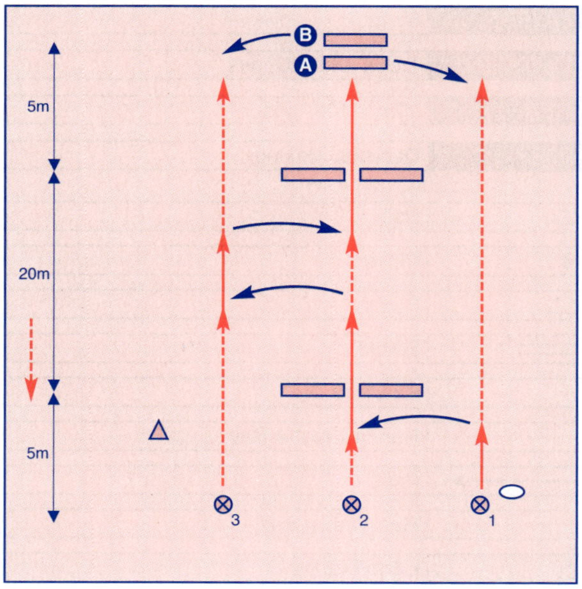

PLAYERS	Minimum 9
EQUIPMENT	6 Shields, 10 Cones and 1 Ball
AREA	30m x 30m grid
AIMS	Decision Making, Support

⬭	Ball
⊗	Player
◠	Bag
▭	Shield
-·-·-·→	Kick/Roll
- - - - →	Run Without a Ball
——→	Pass
——→	Run With a Ball
△	Cone/Marker

Explanation

Player (1) carries the ball and passes to (2). Player (2) busts the shields before off loading to (3). Player (3) adjusts the line, then passes back to (2), who then busts the second set of shields. On busting, Player (2) is confronted with two shields, conditioned by the coach to go for specific players, thus leaving the ball carrier with one of three options, pass to the left or right support, or go it alone.

41

(3 V 2)

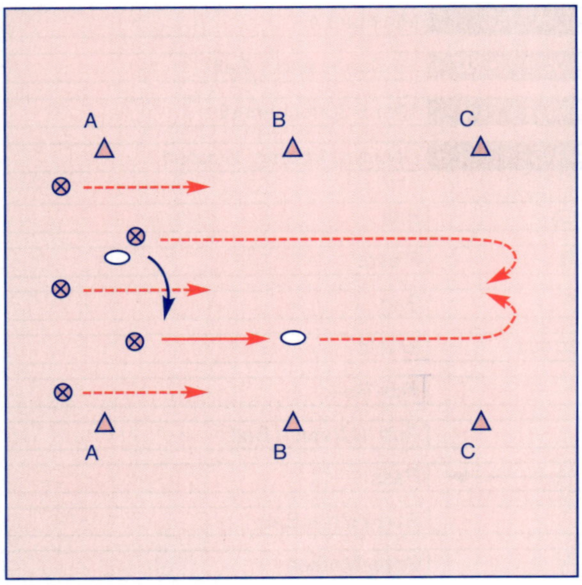

PLAYERS	Minimum 5
EQUIPMENT	1 Ball and 6 Cones
AREA	15m x 15m grids
AIMS	Decision Making

	Ball
	Player
	Bag
	Shield
	Kick/Roll
	Run Without a Ball
	Pass
	Run With a Ball
	Cone/Marker

Explanation

Set out two x 15 metre grids (as above). Using five players in a 3 v 2 formation. All the players stand at the end of the grid (point A). The front players, on the word "Go", proceed down the grid passing the ball. Upon reaching the end of the first grid (Point B), they place the ball down and sprint to point (C) before turning to defend. The team of three players move to pick up the ball as soon as it is placed on the ground, immediately attacking the two defenders. To begin with the defenders place the ball at the centre of point (B), thus creating a 3 v2 ball in the middle situation, but as the attackers become more proficient the ball is placed to the side, 3 v 2 (ball at end).

42

TWO V ONE

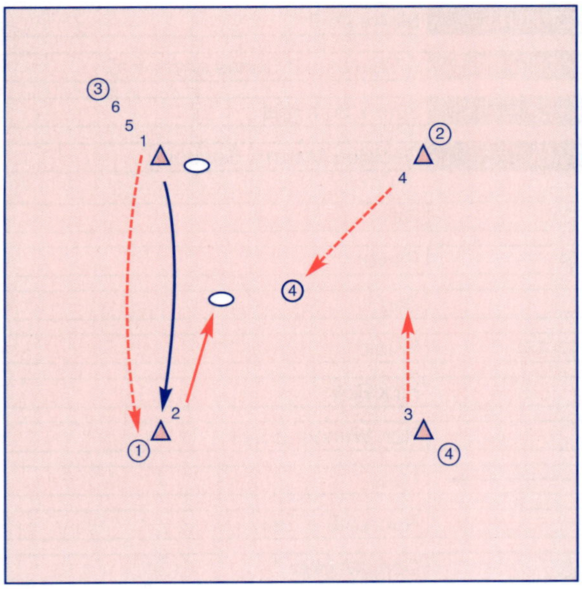

PLAYERS	6
EQUIPMENT	1 Ball and 4 Cones
AREA	10m x 10m grid
AIMS	Decision Making

	Ball
	Player
	Bag
	Shield
	Kick/Roll
	Run Without a Ball
	Pass
	Run With a Ball
	Cone/Marker

Explanation

This is a 2 v 1 continuous drill in a 10m grid (the numbers in squares are secondary positions).

Player (1) begins by throwing a long pass to player (2) and following it. Players (2) and (3) then combine to attack player number (4), in a 2 v 1 situation. On completion (2) now replaces (4) as the defender and (4) becomes the support player. Player number (3) joins the back of players (5) and (6).

NB: This drill gives everyone the opportunity to – a) pass; b) perfect the skill; c) support; d) defend.

The numbers circled on the diagram are the player's secondary positions.

43

2 V 1 DRILL

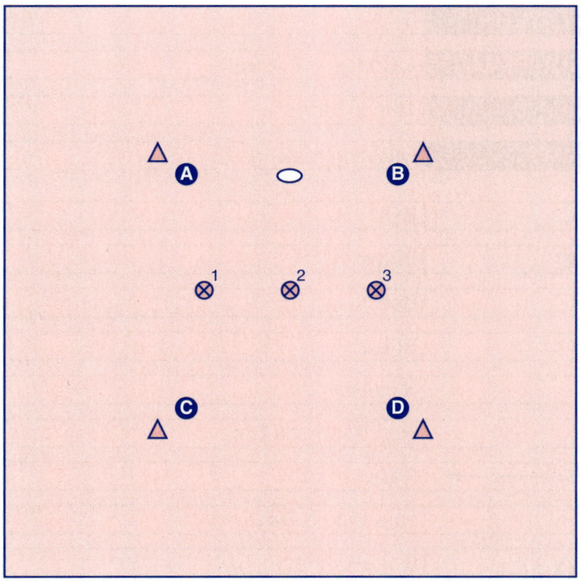

PLAYERS	3
EQUIPMENT	4 Cones and 1 Ball
AREA	10m x 10m grid
AIMS	Decision Making

⬭	Ball
⊗	Player
◠	Bag
▭	Shield
-·-·-→	Kick/Roll
- - - →	Run Without a Ball
——→	Pass
——→	Run With a Ball
△	Cone/Marker

Explanation
A ball is placed on line (AB). Three players line up in the middle of the grid and each is assigned a number (1, 2, 3). The coach shouts out a number. That number designates the defender who must race and touch the line (CD) before turning to confront the other two players who have turned to retrieve the ball from line (AB). The players in possession then attack line (CD) in a normal 2 v 1 situation.

44

DECISION MAKING

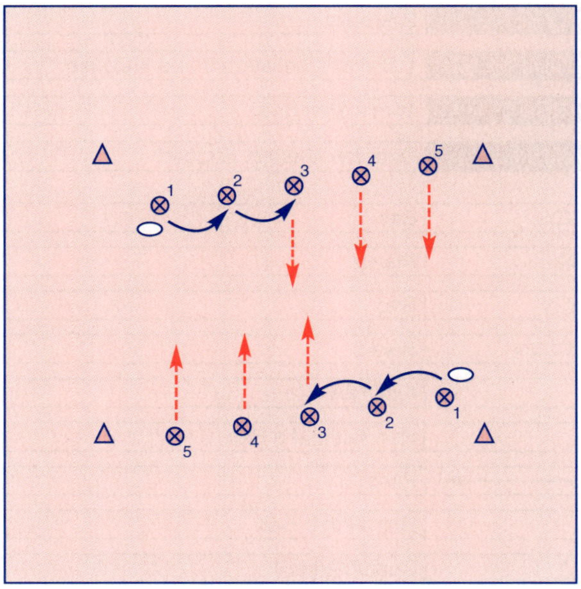

PLAYERS	10
EQUIPMENT	4 Cones and 2 Balls
AREA	20m x 30m grid
AIMS	Decision Making

⬭	Ball
⊗	Player
◠	Bag
▭	Shield
-·-·-→	Kick/Roll
- - - →	Run Without a Ball
——→	Pass
——→	Run With a Ball
△	Cone/Marker

Explanation
Two teams of 5 players line up at opposite ends and across a large grid. The first player in each team has a ball. The two groups run towards each other. Once players (1) and (2) have passed the ball they cease to be attackers and defend against (3), (4) and (5) in the opposing group coming towards them.

45

3 V 3

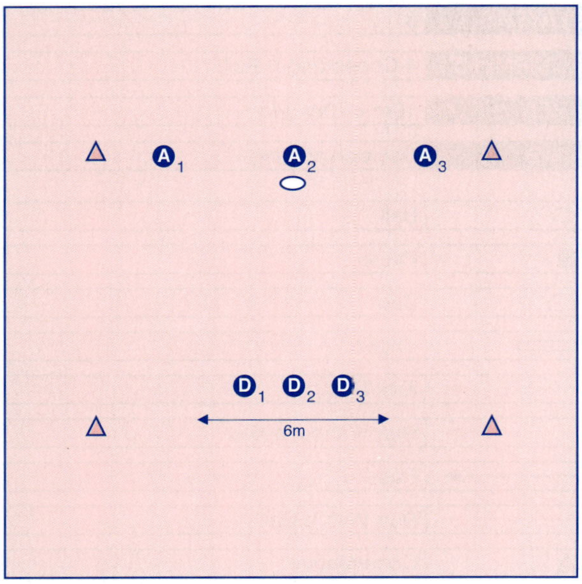

PLAYERS	6
EQUIPMENT	4 Cones and 1 Ball
AREA	15m x 15m grid
AIMS	Decision Making

⬭	Ball
⊗	Player
⌓	Bag
▭	Shield
-·-·-·→	Kick/Roll
------→	Run Without a Ball
——→	Pass
——→	Run With a Ball
△	Cone/Marker

Explanation
3 attackers (A_1, A_2 and A_3) line up across a15m grid. (A_2) is the ball carrier. (A_2) runs directly at (D_1) as he approaches within 3-5m he veers right or left. The attack and defence react accordingly.
It would be expected that the defence would slide with the ball carrier, therefore support runners would need to combine to breach it, i.e: inside ball switches, etc. However, if the defence doesn't slide the ball carrier should make decisions on a wide ball, etc.

46

3 V 2

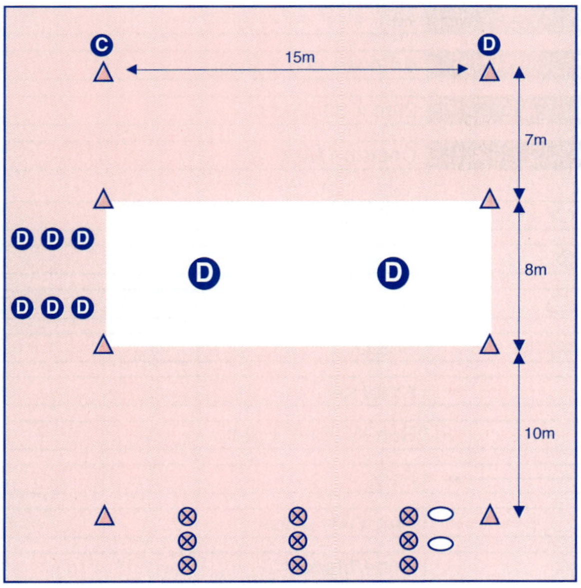

PLAYERS	2 Groups
EQUIPMENT	1 Ball and between 3 and 8 Cones
AREA	15m x 25m grid
AIMS	Decision Making, Support

⬭	Ball
⊗	Player
⌓	Bag
▭	Shield
-·-·-·→	Kick/Roll
------→	Run Without a Ball
——→	Pass
——→	Run With a Ball
△	Cone/Marker

Explanation
This drill lasts for 10 minutes and is competitive. The attackers starting from line AB attempt to score at line CD as many tries as possible (1pt each) in the given time. The defenders working only in the shaded are, attempt to break down each attack by clamping the ball or forcing an error. After each attack, the two defenders are changed, in readiness for the next wave. Attackers must clear the channel immediately they score or breakdown and rejoin the attacking line. Swap the attackers and the defenders after 10 minutes.

47

3 V 2 V 1 V 1

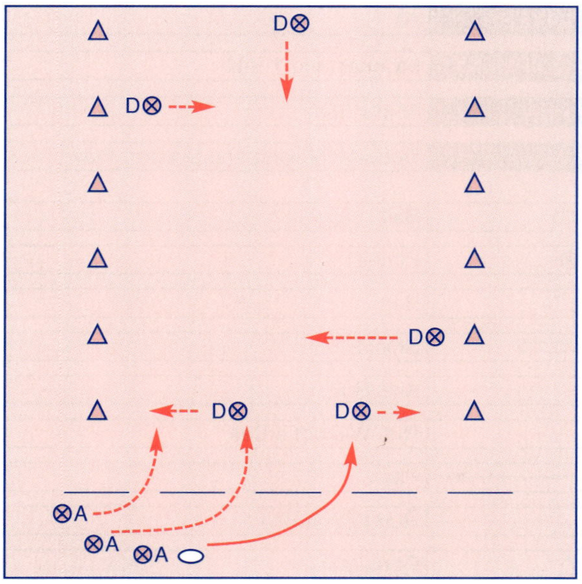

PLAYERS	8
EQUIPMENT	1 Ball and 12 Cones
AREA	15m x 40m
AIMS	Decision Making & Support

	Ball
	Player
	Bag
	Shield
	Kick/Roll
	Run Without a Ball
	Pass
	Run With a Ball
	Cone/Marker

Explanation
3 attackers enter by any gate (entrance) selected by the ball carrier (players either enter by different or same gate depending on coaches instruction). They are immediately confronted by 2 defenders. After negotiating this they meet other defenders fed into the channel. Apart from last defender all others can only move laterally.

48

3 V 2 5 V 2 V 1

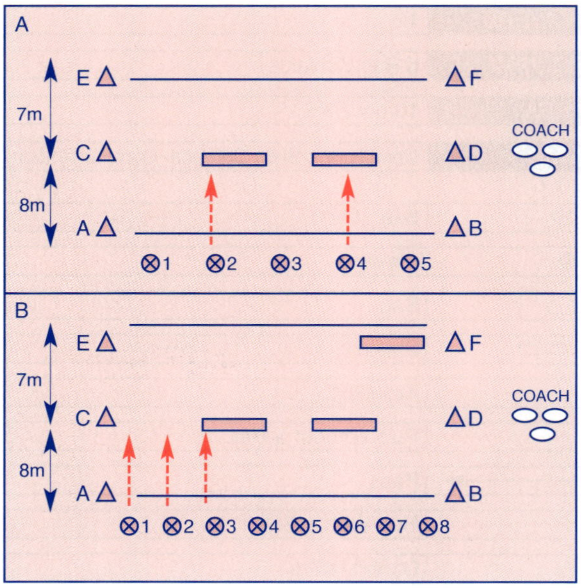

PLAYERS	11
EQUIPMENT	3 Shields, 3 Balls and 6 Cones
AREA	15m x 15m
AIMS	Support/Decision Making

	Ball
	Player
	Bag
	Shield
	Kick/Roll
	Run Without a Ball
	Pass
	Run With a Ball
	Cone/Marker

Explanation

A. 5 players (numbered) lay prone on line A-B. Coach calls our two numbers (e.g: 2&4). They sprint forward & pick up the shields to defend against the other 3 players (who are fed a ball by the coach) who try to score on line E-F.

B. 8 players (numbered) lay prone on line A-B. Coach calls our three numbers (e.g: 1,2&3). They sprint out & pick up the shields (on line E-F & C-D) to defend against other five players (who are fed a ball by the coach) who try to score on line E-F.

49

6 V 4 (SLIDE DRILL)

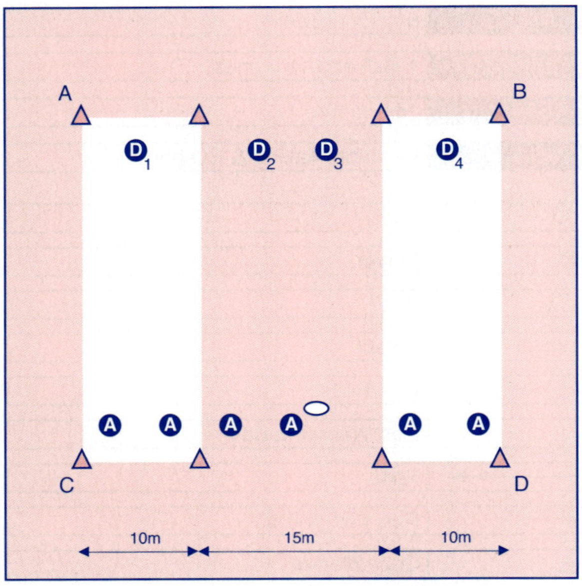

PLAYERS	10
EQUIPMENT	8 Cones and 1 Ball
AREA	35m x 30m
AIMS	Decision Making and Support Play

- Ball
- Player
- Bag
- Shield
- Kick/Roll
- Run Without a Ball
- Pass
- Run With a Ball
- Cone/Marker

Explanation

4 defenders line up to defend line AB. They are restricted in their movements. D2 and D3 can move anywhere in the grid. However D1 can only defend in the 10m channel on the right and nowhere else and likewise D4 can only defend in the 10m channel on the left of the grid and nowhere else. 6 attackers, with a ball, begin from line CD and attempt to score as many tries as possible in 3 minutes. After every try or breakdown, the attackers must restart from line CD. Interchange the defenders each time. The drill is complete.

50

SHIELD AND BAG DRILLS

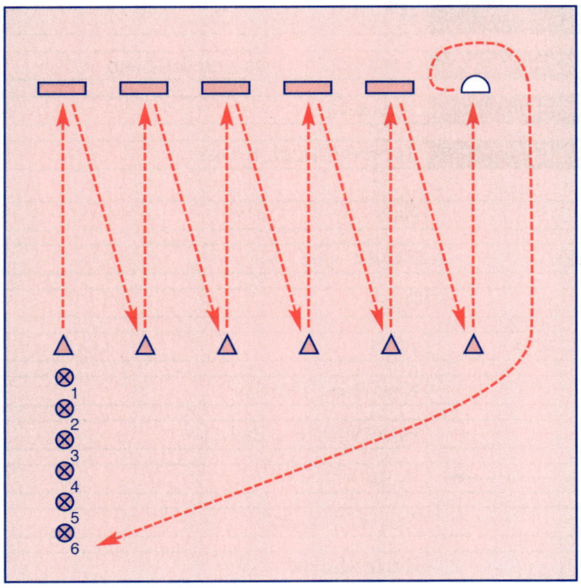

PLAYERS	12
EQUIPMENT	6 Bags/Shields
AREA	10m x 20m
AIMS	Conditioner, Slide Defence, Communication

- Ball
- Player
- Bag
- Shield
- Kick/Roll
- Run Without a Ball
- Pass
- Run With a Ball
- Cone/Marker

Explanation

The practice begins with player (1) moving out to hit and first shield and drifting back to oppose the second shield. Player (1) is now joined by player (2) – they now work together, the drill continues in this manner until all the players have been introduced. The exercise is now complete when the last player has hit the tackle bag, and rejoined his team at the start.

51

BAG DRILL

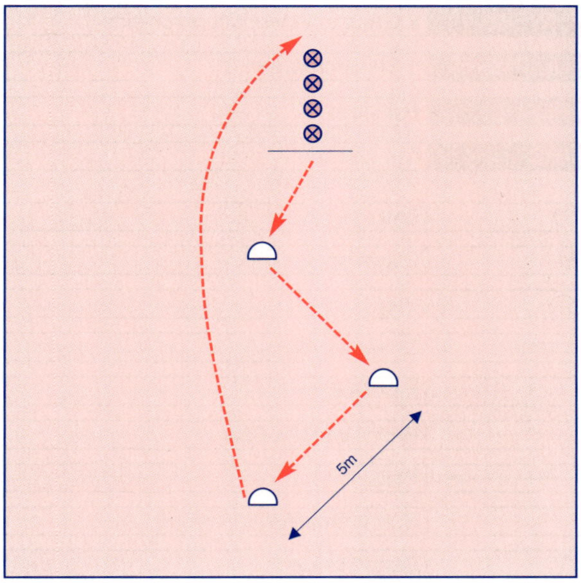

PLAYERS	Minimum 6
EQUIPMENT	4 Cones
AREA	As per diagram
AIMS	Conditioner/Relay

⬭	Ball
⊗	Player
◠	Bag
▭	Shield
-·-·-►	Kick/Roll
--------►	Run Without a Ball
——►	Pass
——►	Run With a Ball
△	Cone/Marker

Explanation
Players are initially required to hold each tackle bag. The remaining players line up at the start line. On "Go" player (1), from behind the start line, runs and tackles the first bag, recovers and picks up the bag thus releasing the former holder to tackle the next bag, etc. Once a player has completed his tackles he then rejoins the drill back at the start line. Encourage players to alternate shoulders.

52

SHIELD (HIT AND SPIN)

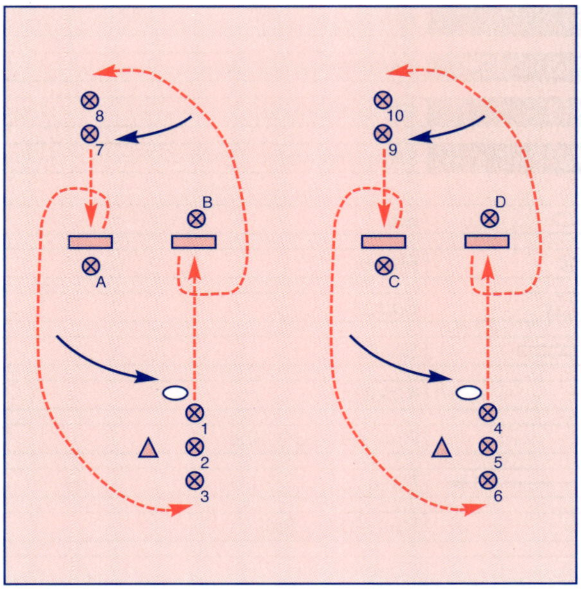

PLAYERS	Minimum 12
EQUIPMENT	4 Shields and 4 Markers
AREA	As per diagram
AIMS	Technique

⬭	Ball
⊗	Player
◠	Bag
▭	Shield
-·-·-►	Kick/Roll
--------►	Run Without a Ball
——►	Pass
——►	Run With a Ball
△	Cone/Marker

Explanation
4 shield holders face the oncoming runners. Each shield is hit simultaneously by one player, who then spins to the right and joins the group to his left. Continue the sequence and switch holder as required.

53

SHIELD DRILL

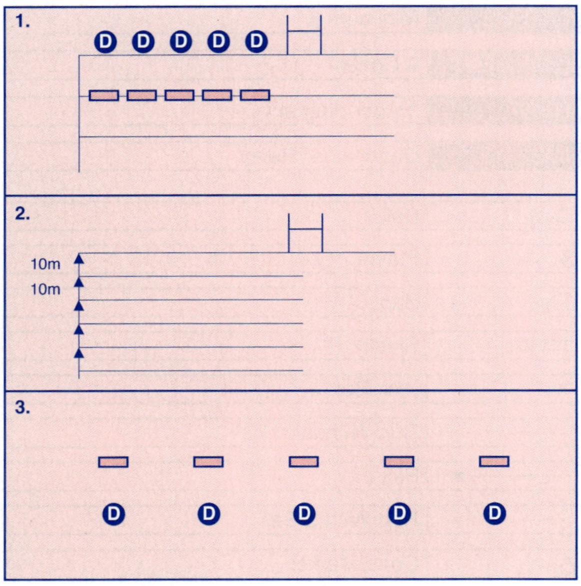

PLAYERS	2 Groups dependant on shields
EQUIPMENT	1 Shield between 2
AREA	Full pitch
AIMS	Conditioner

	Ball
	Player
	Bag
	Shield
	Kick/Roll
	Run Without a Ball
	Pass
	Run With a Ball
	Cone/Marker

Explanation

Mark the field out in 10m intervals from goal-line to goal-line (as in diagram 2). Then line up 5 defenders on the goal-line. Opposite them, 10m away, line up 5 shield carriers (as in diagram 3). On a given signal, the defenders move up together and tackle the shields and force them back a further 10m. The defenders then retreat back 10m.

This takes place all the way up the field to the opposite goal-line.

As the drill continues, the shields should be conditioned to increase their resistance as they get closer to the finish, so that from, say 30% resistance at the beginning, it should be 100% at the end. This increases the pressure on the tackler, who is already suffering from fatigue.

54

BAG DRILL (SLIDE)

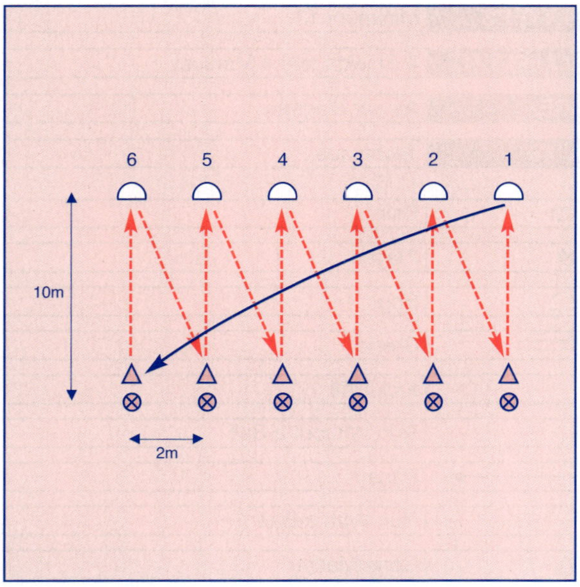

PLAYERS	12
EQUIPMENT	6 Markers and 6 Bags
AREA	10m x 10m grid
AIMS	Slide Defence

	Ball
	Player
	Bag
	Shield
	Kick/Roll
	Run Without a Ball
	Pass
	Run With a Ball
	Cone/Marker

Explanation

6 players line up 10m away from 6 bags. One player will command the line, i.e: call "set" – "up" etc. On command all 6 players go up and tackle the bags as they return the players all slide along to stand opposite the next bag on their right. Except the player who is opposite bag (1) he must track across left and stand opposite bag (6).
The drill continues until everyone returns to their original position.

55

SHIELD DRILL

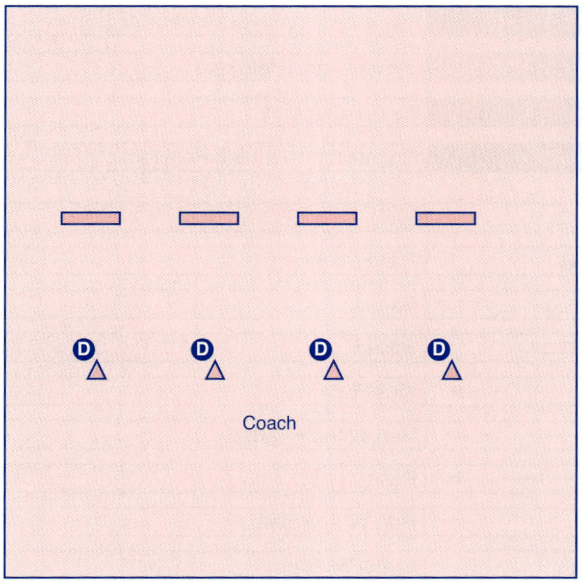

PLAYERS	9
EQUIPMENT	5 Shields and 4 Cones
AREA	10m x 30m
AIMS	Decision Making, Slide Defence

⬭	Ball
⊗	Player
◠	Bag
▭	Shield
–·–·→	Kick/Roll
- - - →	Run Without a Ball
——→	Pass
——→	Run With a Ball
△	Cone/Marker

Explanation

The drill begins with 8 players, 4 defenders and four attackers holding shields. The coach stands behind the defenders and controls the movement of the offence, while the defence reacts to their movements:

a) The coach moves right, the offence follows him, the defenders react accordingly;
b) The coach moves left, the offence follows him, the defenders react accordingly;
c) When the coach moves his hands upwards, the offence jogs forward; the defenders move up in line to hit the shields.

Progression

An extra shield carrier (or player) is added. The coach gives the same signals – however when the offence moves forward one player will always be free! This should always be the shield carrier on the end furthest from the coaches final direction signal.

e.g: If the coach has signalled for the offence to move left and then signals forward (see diagram below). The shield carrier on the right hand side (number 5 in the diagram) should run through unopposed. Shield number 1 would be free if the coach had signalled right before bringing them forward.

It is likely first that:

a) Two defenders will stop the same ball carrier, and
b) A player in the middle will be allowed to penetrate.

As the players begin to think, become aware and communicate, the success of the drill will improve.

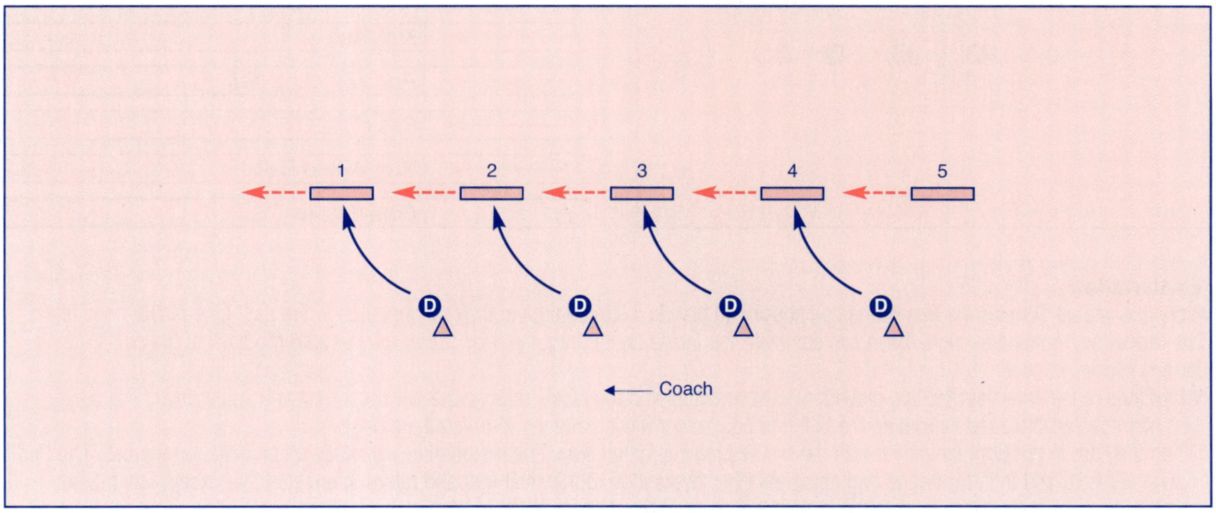

56

BAG DRILL

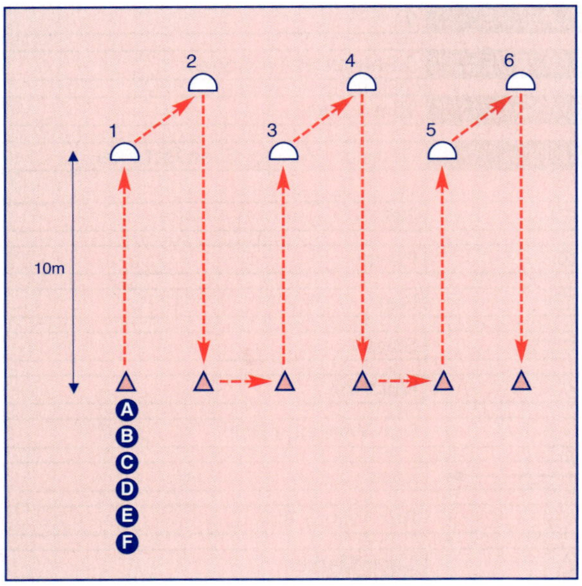

PLAYERS	12
EQUIPMENT	6 Bags and 6 Markers
AREA	As per diagram
AIMS	Regaining Feet (Set Position)

○	Ball
⊗	Player
	Bag
	Shield
	Kick/Roll
	Run Without a Ball
	Pass
	Run With a Ball
△	Cone/Marker

Explanation

6 players line up behind the first marker. He moves forward and tackles Bag (1) and then immediately regains his feet and tackles Bag (2). He then back-pedals to the 2nd marker sliding across to Bag (3). The drill continues with each player making 3 sets of 2 tackles.

57

BAG DRILL

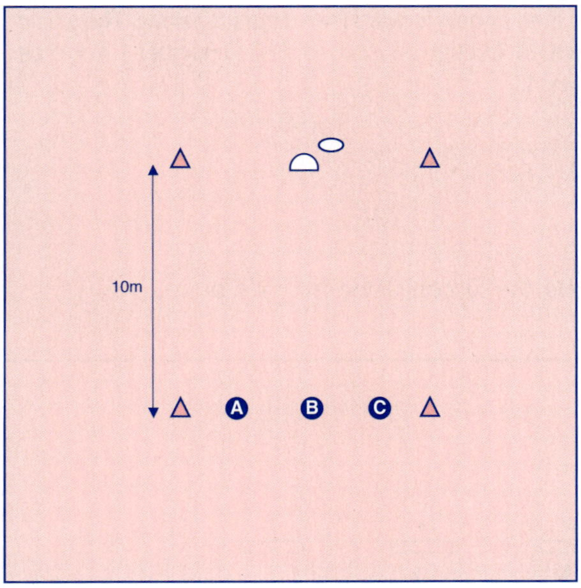

PLAYERS	4
EQUIPMENT	1 Bag, 1 Ball and 3 Cones
AREA	10m x 10m grid
AIMS	Tackle Technique

○	Ball
⊗	Player
	Bag
	Shield
	Kick/Roll
	Run Without a Ball
	Pass
	Run With a Ball
△	Cone/Marker

Explanation

3 players line up 10m from a bag with a ball positioned behind it. On command they run forwards to the bag. One player nominates low tackle, one nominates high, these two complete the tackle on the bag, the third player runs around the back of the bag to cover for any slipped passes.

When they regain their feet the two players who have completed the tackle take up the position of 1st and 2nd marker. The player who has covered the pass – picks up the ball (the bag holder having already re-erected the bag).

When they are in position, the player with the ball will roll it to either side. The first marker will chase off and dive on the ball. The 2nd marker will hold and then tackle the bag again. All the players then regain their feet and return to the start line except first marker who retrieves the ball, places back down, erects the bag and the drill continues.

58

BAG DRILL (SLIDE)

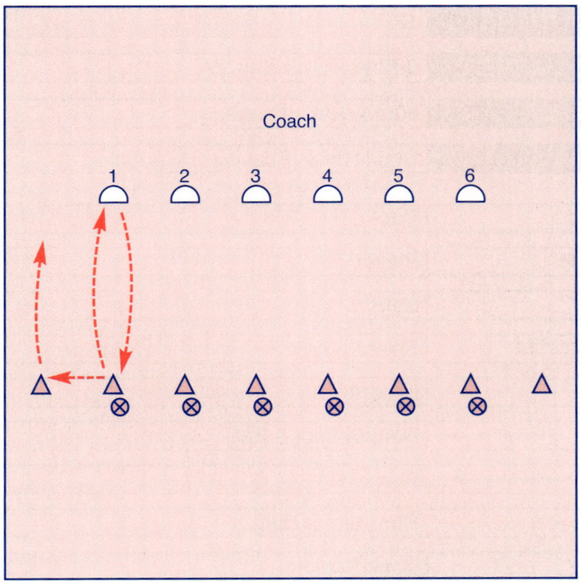

PLAYERS	12
EQUIPMENT	6 Bags and 8 Markers
AREA	10m x 20m grid
AIMS	Slide Defence, Technique

Explanation

6 players stand opposite 6 bags, 10m away. On command from the coach who puts up his arms to signal a 'play the ball' they run up and tackle the bag opposite them.They then return to their marker but slide to the next marker to their left. On the same command from their coach they come forward and tackle the same bag as before, but on an angle.

They then return to their original mark and slide to the next cone to the right and await the coaches signal.

After 6 tackles change the tacklers.

59

SLIDE DRILLS

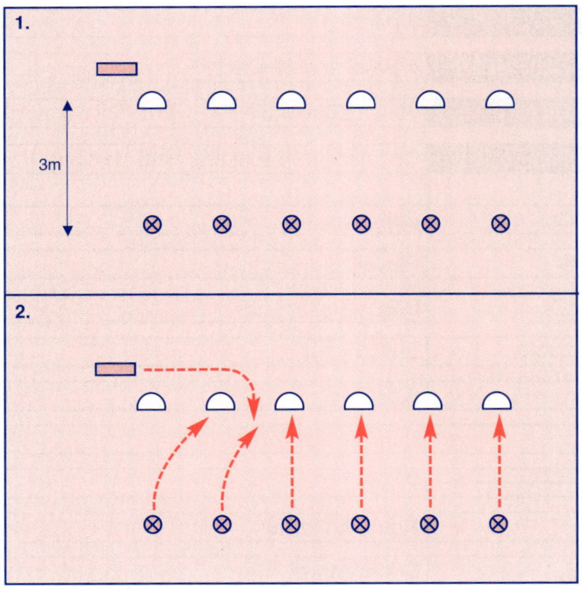

PLAYERS	13
EQUIPMENT	6 Bags and 1 Shield
AREA	20m x 3m
AIMS	Slide Defence, Decision Making

Explanation

6 players line up 3m away from and opposite a bag and begin running on the spot. A shield carrier runs along the back of the line. He is allowed to come into the line anywhere between the bags. The line must adjust to take him. Continue for 6 tackles (see diagram 2).

60

CONTACT DRILL

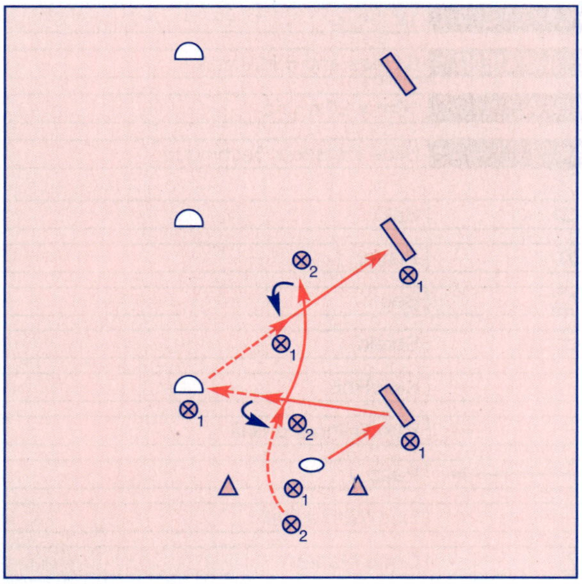

PLAYERS	16
EQUIPMENT	3 Bags and 3 Shields
AREA	20m x 10m channel
AIMS	Conditioner, Passing, Hit & Spin

	Ball
	Player
	Bag
	Shield
	Kick/Roll
	Run Without a Ball
	Pass
	Run With a Ball
	Cone/Marker

Explanation

In pairs. Player (1) runs to first pad, hits and spins, off loads to player (2) who is in support. He then runs and tackles the first bag. He regains his feet and receives a pass from player (2). He then repeats the drill all the way up the channel.

After completing the channel, swap roles so that each player has a chance to take part.

61

TACKLE BAGS

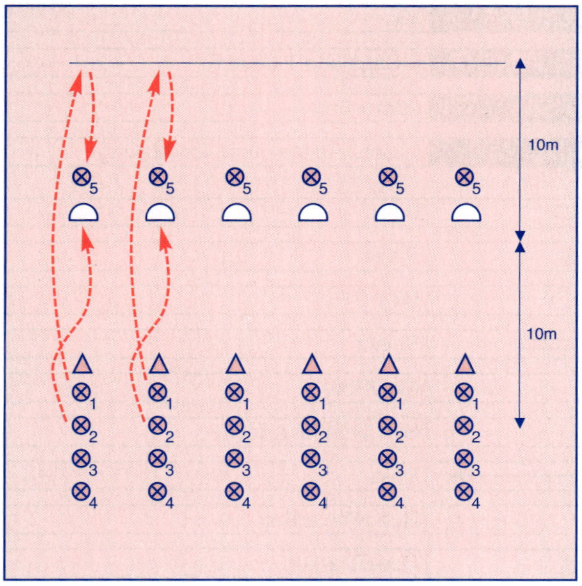

PLAYERS	5 per bag
EQUIPMENT	4 Bags and 12 Cones
AREA	20m x 20m grid
AIMS	Conditioner, Regaining Feet, Timing

	Ball
	Player
	Bag
	Shield
	Kick/Roll
	Run Without a Ball
	Pass
	Run With a Ball
	Cone/Marker

Explanation

1st player runs out to the far line (20m) touches, turns and comes back. The 2nd player in the line runs out and tackles the bag, regains his feet and picks it up for player (1) to tackle on his way back, thus releasing player (5) to join back of line after tackling. Player (1) then regains his feet and holds up the bag. Player (3) runs to the far line whilst player (4) runs up and tackles the bag and the drill continues.

62

TACKLE CIRCUIT

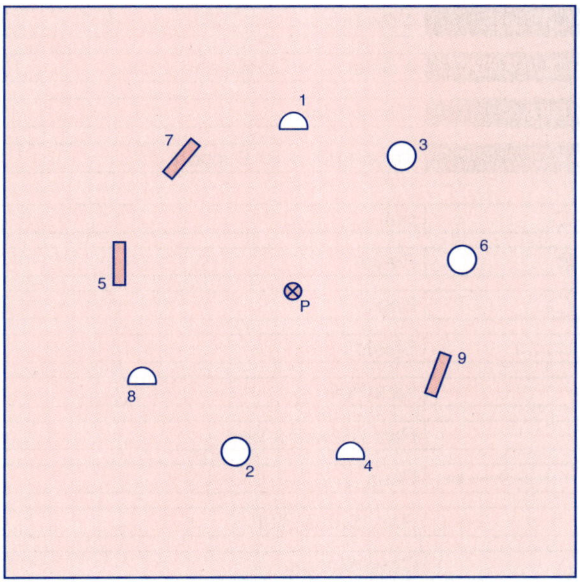

PLAYERS	10 (dependant on equipment)
EQUIPMENT	2 Tubes, 3 Shields and 3 Bags ‡
AREA	10m circle
AIMS	Conditioner

⬭	Ball
⊗	Player
⌓	Bag
▭	Shield
–·–·–·→	Kick/Roll
---------→	Run Without a Ball
——→	Pass
——→	Run With a Ball
△	Cone/Marker

Explanation

Form equipment in a 10m diameter circle around a player (P). The player works for a period of time specified by the coach, tackling the equipment around him. He must alternate shoulders after each tackle. The player responds to calls from the equipment holders. He must knock down bags, force back oncoming shields and hit through inner-tubes rolled towards him.

‡ Permutate available equipment.

63

BAG DRILL

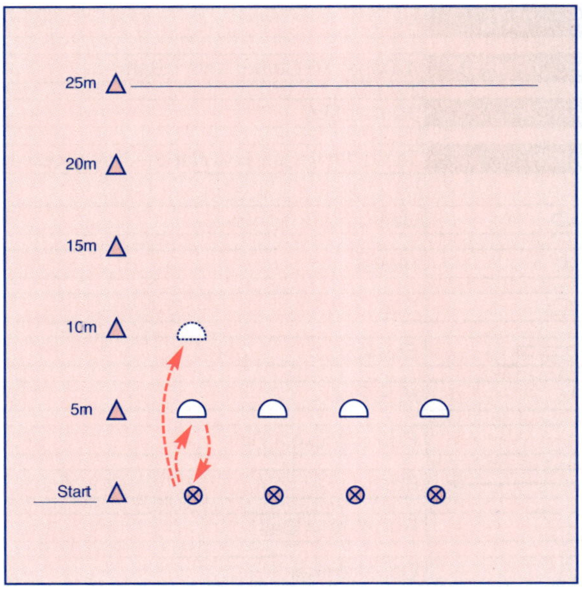

PLAYERS	8 (dependant on number of bags)
EQUIPMENT	4 Bags and 16 Cones
AREA	25m x 20m
AIMS	Conditioner

⬭	Ball
⊗	Player
⌓	Bag
▭	Shield
–·–·–·→	Kick/Roll
---------→	Run Without a Ball
——→	Pass
——→	Run With a Ball
△	Cone/Marker

Explanation

Four players on the start line move forward and hit bags at the 5m then retreat to the start line. The bag holders then take bags back to the 10m line.The bags are hit again and tacklers return to the start or the bags are taken to the 10m line. The tacklers are still working as a team unit move forward and again make a tackle and return to the start line together. Thereafter the players work at their own pace with bags being taken 5m at a time. On reaching the 25m mark the players make two tackles at 25m before the bag holders bring the bags back down the ladder, i.e: the tackle sequence is 5m, 10m, 15m, 20m, 25m, 20m, 15m, etc. This drill is timed for 5 minutes with a count of tackles made, kept for each player. A target of 24 is regarded as quite good in this period.

64

SHIELD DRILL

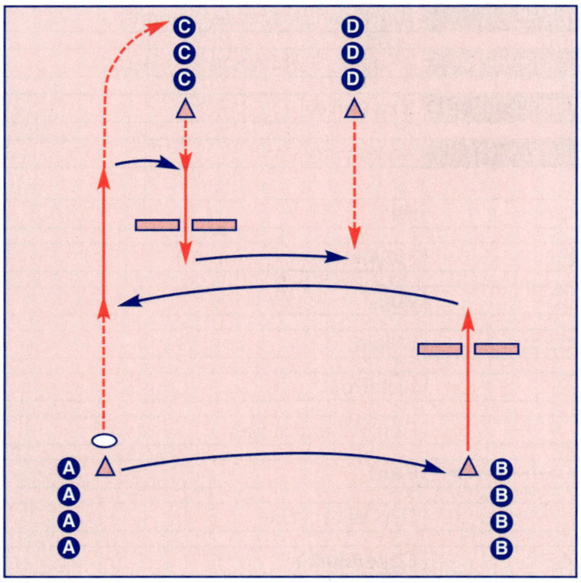

PLAYERS	4 Groups
EQUIPMENT	4 Shields, 4 Cones and 1 Ball
AREA	15m x 15m
AIMS	Passing (L & S) Support

⬭	Ball
⊗	Player
⌓	Bag
▭	Shield
–·–·–·→	Kick/Roll
- - - - →	Run Without a Ball
——→ (blue)	Pass
——→ (red)	Run With a Ball
△	Cone/Marker

Explanation

A gives long ball to (B)
B busts shields and returns ball to (A)
A gives short ball to (C)
C BUSTS and passes to (D)
D passes short to (B)
B bursts
B long to (A), etc.
A short pass to (C)

65

QUICKHAND/DRIFT DEFENCE

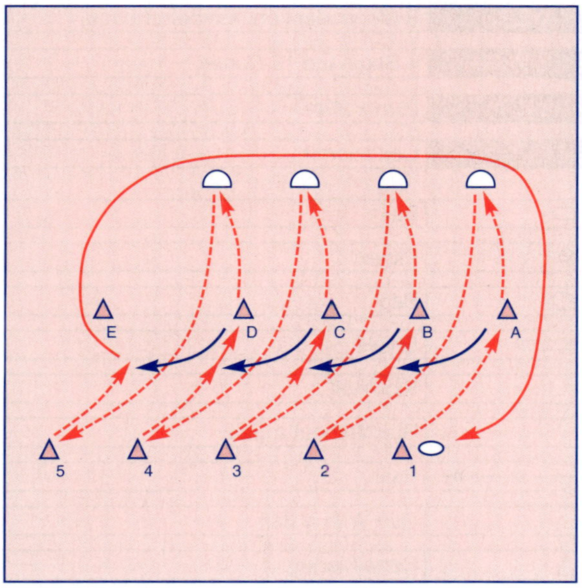

PLAYERS	9
EQUIPMENT	4 Bags, 10 Cones and 1 Ball
AREA	10m x 20m
AIMS	Tackle Technique, Fast Hands, Slide Defence

⬭	Ball
⊗	Player
⌓	Bag
▭	Shield
–·–·–·→	Kick/Roll
- - - - →	Run Without a Ball
——→ (blue)	Pass
——→ (red)	Run With a Ball
△	Cone/Marker

Explanation

Player 1 begins with the ball at the first cone. He approaches cone A and passes to player 2 who is supporting. On passing, player 1 then drifts left and tackles bag 1 before back pedalling to player 2's original position. The drill is repeated along the line until player 4 passes to player 5. Player 4 tackles bag 4 and back pedals into player 5's position, but player 5 on collecting the ball runs around cone E and the back of the bags to restart the drill from the beginning.

66

KICKING

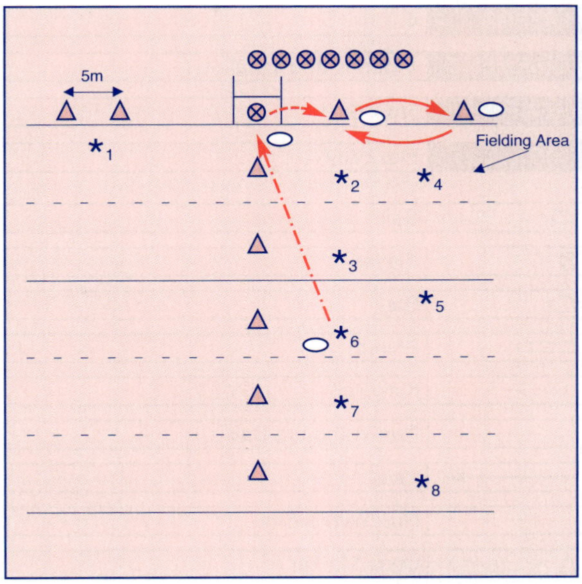

PLAYERS	2 Teams (minimum 16)
EQUIPMENT	3 Balls and 9 Cones
AREA	Half Field
AIMS	Kicking, Regaining Possession, Fast Hands

	Ball
	Player
	Bag
	Shield
	Kick/Roll
	Run Without a Ball
	Pass
	Run With a Ball
	Cone/Marker

Explanation

Set out as above, with kickers (X) and fielders (*). Any type of kick may be used into the fielding area.
A run is scored by kicking, picking up the ball at (A), touching down at (B), picking up a second ball at (B) and scoring at (A).
Batting (kicking) players can be caught out or run out by fielders making five consecutive passes ending with Player (1) touching down between the cones.

NB: Size of teams and number of passes can be altered.

67

KICKING TENNIS

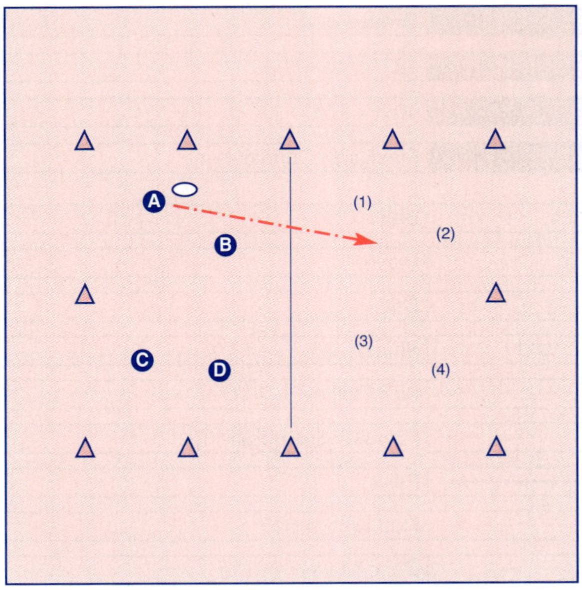

PLAYERS	8
EQUIPMENT	12 Markers and 1 Ball
AREA	40m x 20m grid
AIMS	Kicking, Regaining Possession

	Ball
	Player
	Bag
	Shield
	Kick/Roll
	Run Without a Ball
	Pass
	Run With a Ball
	Cone/Marker

Explanation

Two teams, four against four, in a 40m x 20m area with one team in each half, as in the diagram above.
Player (A) starts the game by kicking the ball into the other half. If the ball goes out of bounds, without a bounce, the servers lose a point. The receivers have to control the ball quickly. All punts must be caught cleanly before the ball touches the ground. Grubber-kicks should be controlled immediately. The kickers receive one point if the receivers knock on, or if the ball bounces before going out of the grid. The ball is kicked back and the game continues.

68

AGILITY SQUARE

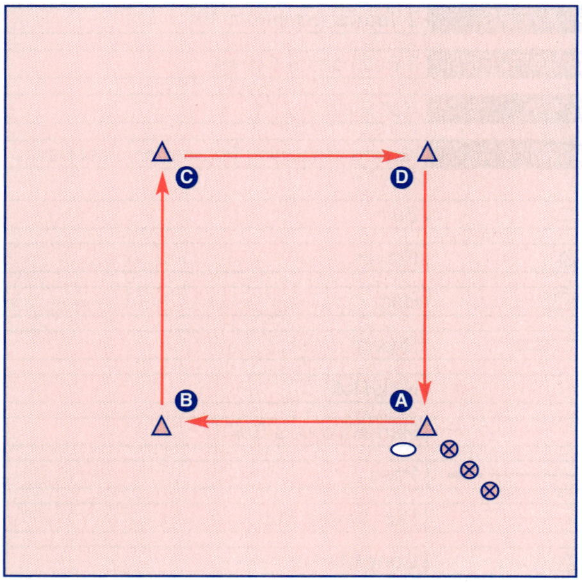

PLAYERS	4
EQUIPMENT	4 Cones and 1 Ball
AREA	5m x 5m
AIMS	Flexibility

⬭	Ball
⊗	Player
⌓	Bag
▭	Shield
–·–·–·→	Kick/Roll
----------→	Run Without a Ball
——→ (blue)	Pass
——→ (red)	Run With a Ball
△	Cone/Marker

Explanation

Players line up behind cone(A). First player with a ball slides to the left to cone (B). He then back pedals to cone (C), slides right to cone (D) before sprinting back to (A). The ball is handed to the next player who repeats and the drill continues. This drill is done at pace. Several grids can be set up and an element of competition can be brought in.

As an extension cones can be placed between (D) and (A) causing the player to step in and out.

69

AGILITY DRILL

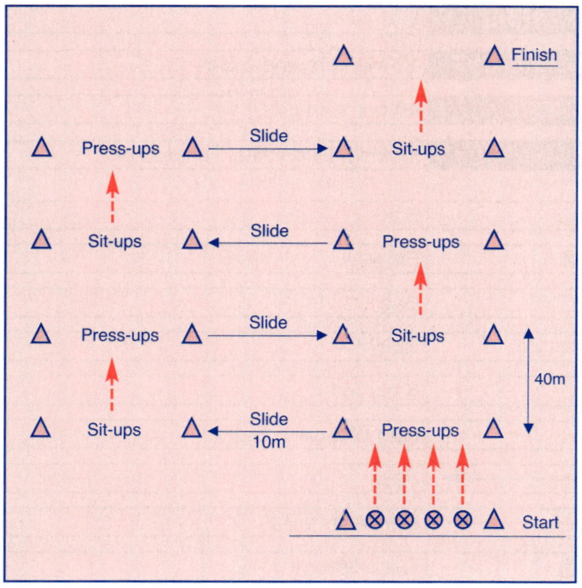

PLAYERS	Groups of 4
EQUIPMENT	18 Cones
AREA	40m x 20m
AIMS	Flexibility, Conditioner

⬭	Ball
⊗	Player
⌓	Bag
▭	Shield
–·–·–·→	Kick/Roll
----------→	Run Without a Ball
——→ (blue)	Pass
——→ (red)	Run With a Ball
△	Cone/Marker

Explanation

In teams of 4. First group run forward as a unit – hit the floor 5 press-ups slide left 10m and hit the floor and do 5 sit-ups. They run forward and hit the floor for 5 press-ups before sliding right. The group then follow a similar pattern to the end. On finishing the drill the group jogs back to the start.

NB: This drill is done at pace with each group completing 6 runs before resting.

70

AGILITY DRILL

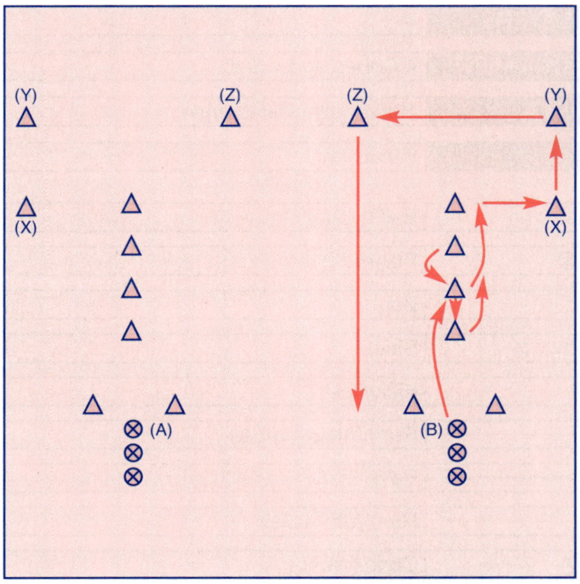

PLAYERS	2 Groups of 4
EQUIPMENT	18 Cones
AREA	25m x 30m
AIMS	Flexibility

⬭	Ball
⊗	Player
⌓	Bag
▭	Shield
-·-·-·-→	Kick/Roll
- - - - →	Run Without a Ball
——→	Pass
——→	Run With a Ball
△	Cone/Marker

Explanation
This is a competition between two groups of 4. On the coaches command, the ball carrier moves up to the 2nd cone and back pedals to the 1st. He then goes forward 2 more cones and back pedals one. He then goes forward two more before back pedalling one. He runs forward one and slides sideways to cone (X). He then runs forward to cone (Y), slides sideways to cone (Z) and sprints forward to trigger the next runner by handing over the ball.

71

AGILITY DRILL

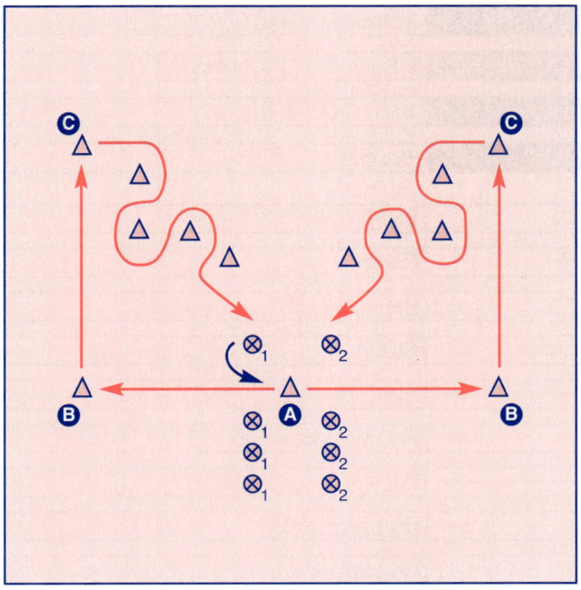

PLAYERS	2 Groups of 4
EQUIPMENT	12 Cones and 2 Balls
AREA	10m x 10m grid
AIMS	Flexibility

⬭	Ball
⊗	Player
⌓	Bag
▭	Shield
-·-·-·-→	Kick/Roll
- - - - →	Run Without a Ball
——→	Pass
——→	Run With a Ball
△	Cone/Marker

Explanation
2 players, holding balls, face each other at cone (A). The drill begins when player (1) decides to move.
The players back pedal to cone (B) before sliding sideways to (C). At cone (C) they run forward in and out of the cones before handing over to the next player in their team who continues. The winning team is the first to complete 4 runs.
NB: When the players run forwards around cones they must change hands with the ball as if fending off the cone.

72

AGILITY DRILL

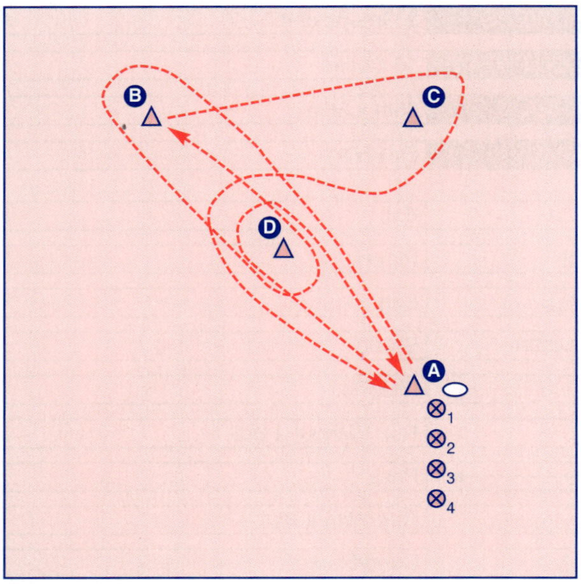

PLAYERS	4
EQUIPMENT	4 Cones and 1 Ball
AREA	10m equilateral triangle
AIMS	Flexibility

⬭	Ball
⊗	Player
◠	Bag
▭	Shield
-·-·->	Kick/Roll
------>	Run Without a Ball
——>	Pass
——>	Run With a Ball
△	Cone/Marker

Explanation
4 cones are placed in a triangular formation. Player (1), carrying a ball begins from cone (A). He runs forward and goes around cone (D) and back pedals around his own cone before running forward to cone (B). He goes around cone (B) and runs forward to touch cone (D) and back pedals to (B) before running forwards to cone (C) then runs around it to cone (D) where he, on touching the cone, back pedals to the start at cone (A). He then delivers a pass to the next player.

73

AGILITY DRILLS

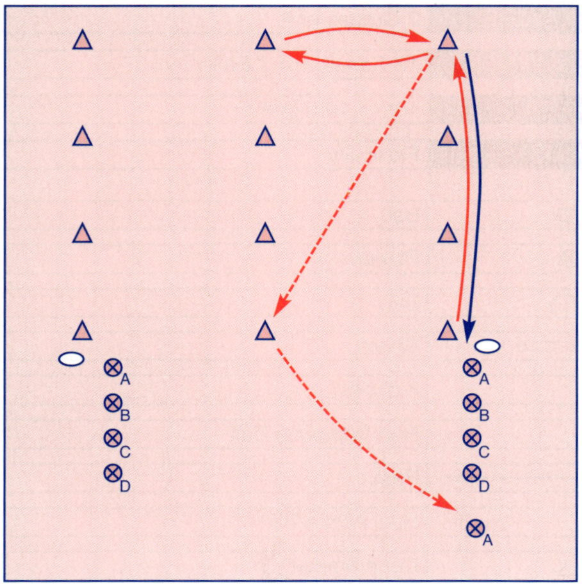

PLAYERS	2 Groups of 4
EQUIPMENT	2 Balls and 12 Cones
AREA	10m x 10m grid
AIMS	Flexibility

⬭	Ball
⊗	Player
◠	Bag
▭	Shield
-·-·->	Kick/Roll
------>	Run Without a Ball
——>	Pass
——>	Run With a Ball
△	Cone/Marker

Explanation
This is a progressive drill. Both lines start together. The front man (A) carrying a ball runs up the line of cones to the end. Moves sideways across to the middle cone then slides back and delivers a pass to (B) who follows the same pattern. (A) then back pedals diagonally to the middle cone on the start line and then rejoins the back of his group.

Progressions: On his 2nd run, a player would run in and out of the cones on the way up before completing the drill as normal. On 3rd run he would run completely around the cones whilst running forward before completing the drill as normal.

74

MOBILITY

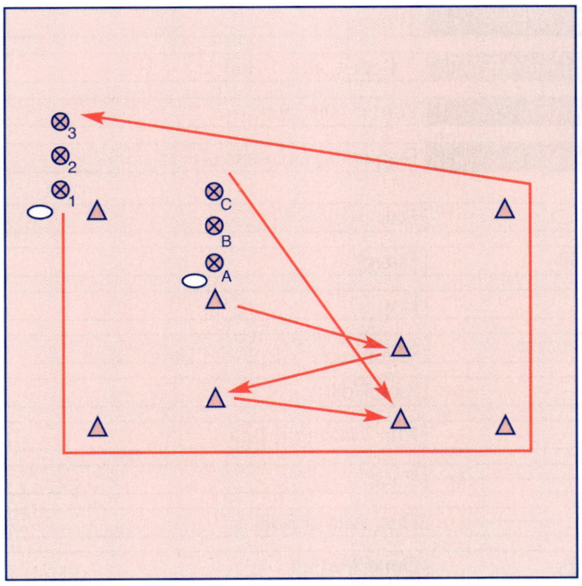

PLAYERS	6 or 8
EQUIPMENT	8 Cones and 2 Balls
AREA	6m x 6m grid
AIMS	Flexibility

⬭	Ball
⊗	Player
⌓	Bag
▭	Shield
–·–·–·→	Kick/Roll
- - - - →	Run Without a Ball
——→	Pass
——→	Run With a Ball
△	Cone/Marker

Explanation
Use teams of three or four players in a 6 metre grid. Each player in turn runs with a ball. One team runs around the grid, the other team runs in a zig-zag fashion as shown in the diagram. The first team to have all their players home wins the game.

75

AGILITY

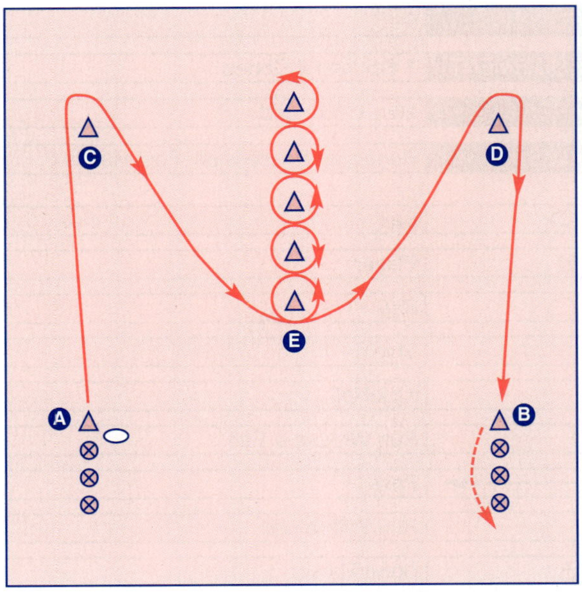

PLAYERS	6
EQUIPMENT	9 Cones and 1 Ball
AREA	10m x 20m
AIMS	Agility Running

⬭	Ball
⊗	Player
⌓	Bag
▭	Shield
–·–·–·→	Kick/Roll
- - - - →	Run Without a Ball
——→	Pass
——→	Run With a Ball
△	Cone/Marker

Explanation
Two groups of 3 players line up behind cones (A) and (B). The first player from (A) runs to cone (C) and then down to cone (E). He then runs in and out of the cones up and back before running around cone (D) and joining the back of the other group. This triggers off the lead runner from group (B) who follows the same pattern in the opposite direction. The drill continues.

76

REGAINING POSSESSION

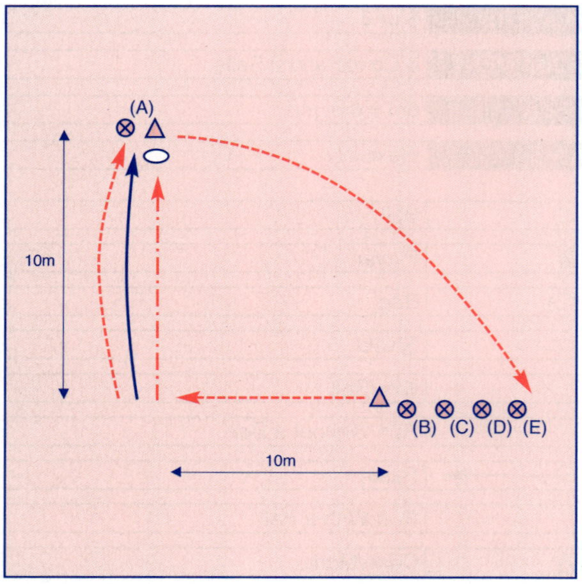

PLAYERS	Minimum 4
EQUIPMENT	2 Cones and 1 Ball
AREA	10m x 10m grid
AIMS	Regaining Possession

	Ball
	Player
	Bag
	Shield
	Kick/Roll
	Run Without a Ball
	Pass
	Run With a Ball
	Cone/Marker

Explanation
Players line up by the cone as shown. Player (A) rolls the ball and (B) has to pick it up whilst both he and the ball are moving. He then passes back to (A) who places on the ground then joins the end of the line as (B) takes his place. The drill continues.

77

HANDLING/MOBILITY

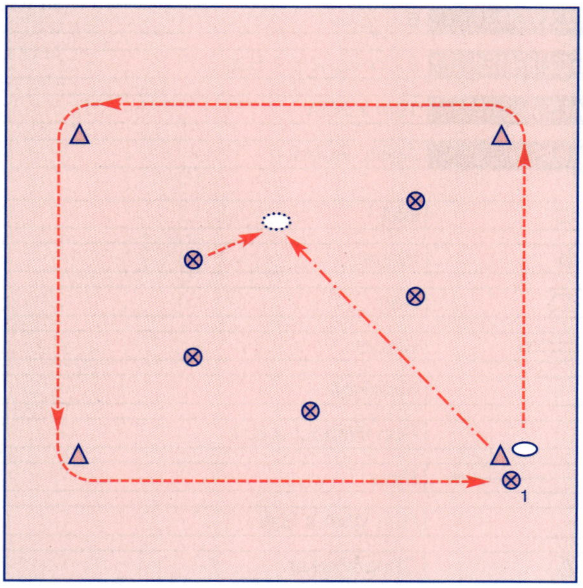

PLAYERS	6
EQUIPMENT	1 Ball and 4 Cones
AREA	20m x 20m grid
AIMS	Regaining Possession, Fast Hands

	Ball
	Player
	Bag
	Shield
	Kick/Roll
	Run Without a Ball
	Pass
	Run With a Ball
	Cone/Marker

Explanation
Player (1) rolls the ball as hard as possible into the grid and then runs around the outside of the four markers.
The five defenders regain possession and pass to each other in turn.
The player who catches the last pass attempts to touch the start marker before the runner arrives home.
The players take it in turn to roll out the ball. One point is scored for each successful circuit.

78

REGAINING POSSESSION

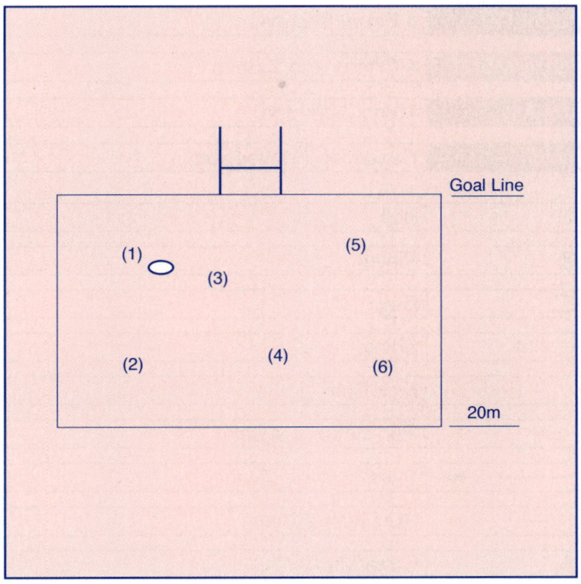

PLAYERS	4 to 8
EQUIPMENT	1 Ball
AREA	20m x 60m
AIMS	Taking a High Ball

⬭	Ball
⊗	Player
⌓	Bag
▭	Shield
-·-·-·→	Kick/Roll
- - - - →	Run Without a Ball
——→	Pass
——→	Run With a Ball
△	Cone/Marker

Explanation
A group of players is spread in an area approximately one quarter of the playing field. Each player is given a number. One player kicks the ball high and calls a number. The player whose number is called must run and catch the kick. That player immediately kicks the ball high and calls another number. Each player has a number of lives and they lose one life:

a) for each kick which lands out of bounds, and
b) for each dropped ball

79

REGAINING POSSESSION AHB

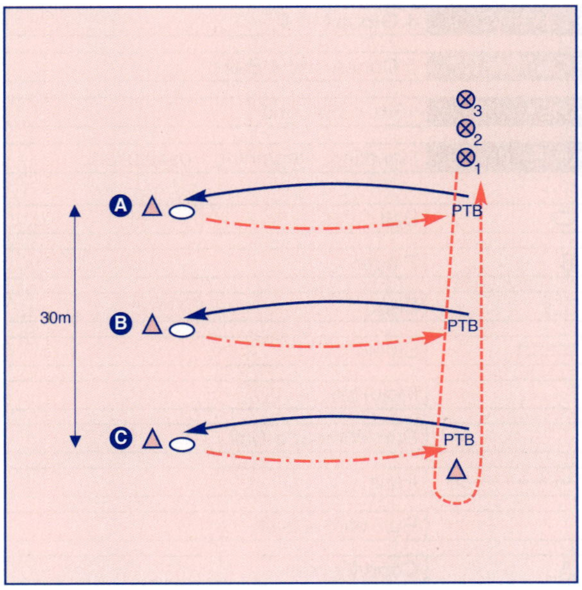

PLAYERS	6
EQUIPMENT	4 Markers and 3 Balls
AREA	As per diagram
AIMS	Regaining Possession, Fast PTB, Good pass from the floor

⬭	Ball
⊗	Player
⌓	Bag
▭	Shield
-·-·-·→	Kick/Roll
- - - - →	Run Without a Ball
——→	Pass
——→	Run With a Ball
△	Cone/Marker

Explanation
Two teams of three players (as per diagram). Players (A), (B) and (C) placed 5 metres apart, have a ball each. Player (1) runs forward and dives on the ball rolled out by player (A). Player (1) on regaining his feet, plays the ball backwards. He runs forwards and repeats the process at (B) and (C). He then runs around the marker and returns, picking up each ball and passing dummy half style to the player who originally rolled it out to him.

80

SQUARE DRILL

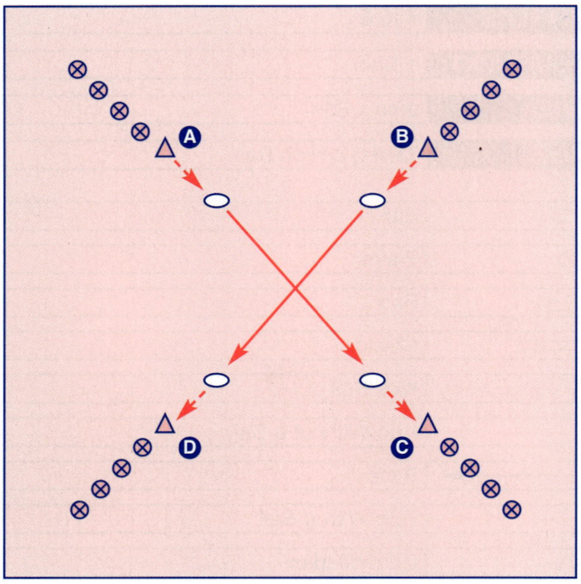

PLAYERS	4 Equal Groups
EQUIPMENT	4 Cones and 2 Balls
AREA	10m x 10m grid
AIMS	Regaining Possession

⬭	Ball
⊗	Player
⌓	Bag
▭	Shield
-·-·-·→	Kick/Roll
- - - - →	Run Without a Ball
——→	Pass
——→	Run With a Ball
△	Cone/Marker

Explanation
Players in four groups at grid corners. (A) and (B) start with a ball placed 1-2 metres in front of them.
The two players (A) and (B) on the word "Go" pick up the ball on the run, then place it down 1-2 metres in front of (C) and (D). Players (C) and (D) continue the drill by regaining possession and placing the ball down in front of files (A) and (B), etc.

81

REGAINING POSSESSION

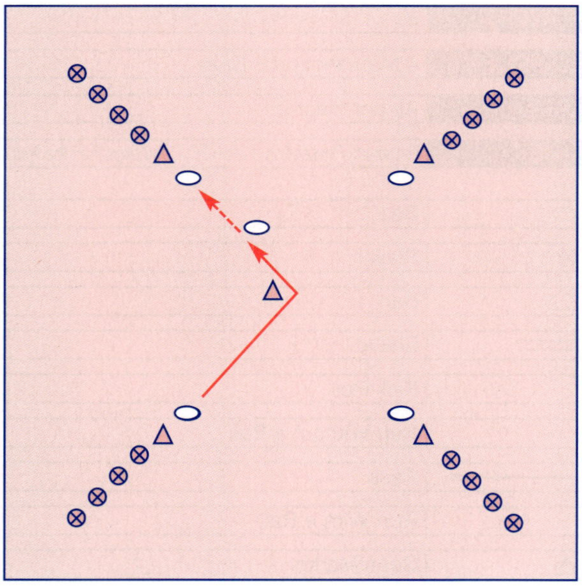

PLAYERS	4 Groups of 4
EQUIPMENT	5 Cones and 4 Balls
AREA	15m x 15m grid
AIMS	Handling, Regaining Possession

⬭	Ball
⊗	Player
⌓	Bag
▭	Shield
-·-·-·→	Kick/Roll
- - - - →	Run Without a Ball
——→	Pass
——→	Run With a Ball
△	Cone/Marker

Explanation
Three or four players and a ball in each corner. On the word "Go", all four ball carriers run to the centre marker and turn anticlockwise, scoring by placing the ball down halfway towards the next corner. The second player from each team then begins his run, picks up the ball, runs to the centre, turns anticlockwise and scores, etc.

82

PASS OUT OF TACKLE

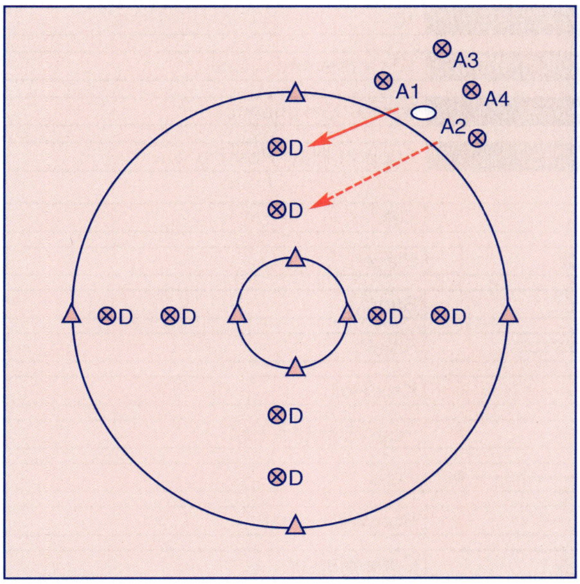

PLAYERS	16
EQUIPMENT	8 Balls and 8 Cones
AREA	10m (Diam) circle
AIMS	Support play/pass out of tackle

	Ball
	Player
	Bag
	Shield
	Kick/Roll
	Run Without a Ball
	Pass
	Run With a Ball
	Cone/Marker

Explanation

D's are defenders in pairs. A1 & A2 enter circle with a ball. A1 attempts to break through 1st pair of defenders and offload to A2 in the tackle. A2 then attempts to break through next pair & offload in the tackle to A1 who has supported him. After 10 secs next 2 attackers A3 & A4 enter. After 90 secs reverse roles. After 90 secs reverse directions.

***Note:** Gum shields necessary*

83

PASS OUT OF TACKLE

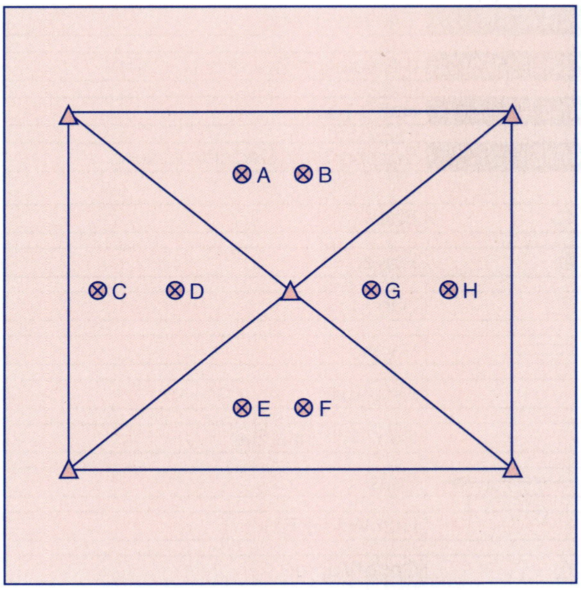

PLAYERS	8
EQUIPMENT	5 Cones and 1 Ball
AREA	8m x 8m grid
AIMS	Passing, decision making & conditioning

	Ball
	Player
	Bag
	Shield
	Kick/Roll
	Run Without a Ball
	Pass
	Run With a Ball
	Cone/Marker

Explanation

Team 1: A, C, E, G. Team 2: B, D, F, H.

Each pair work within 8 x 5 triangle. Team 1 begin with the ball and have 90 secs to see how many passes around the grid. A tries to pass to C whilst being tackled by B. As soon as C has the ball D moves into tackle etc.
If a defender clamps the ball for more than 3 secs a release call is made and the ball is passed on to the next attacker. Change roles after 90 secs. Change direction next time round.

***Note:** Gum shields necessary*

84

SUPPORT

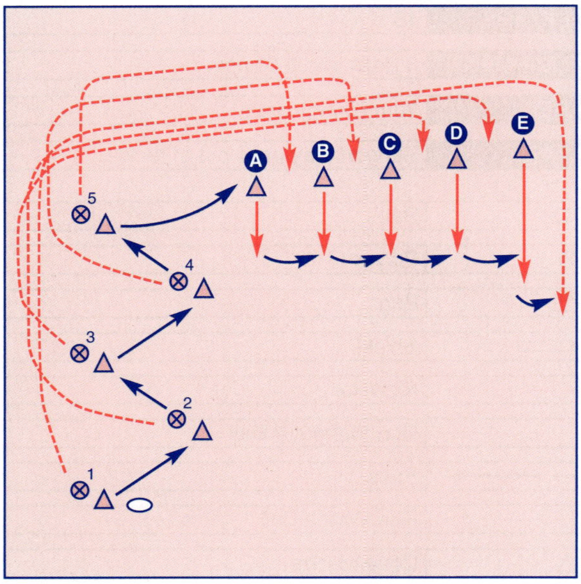

PLAYERS	10
EQUIPMENT	10 Cones and 1 Ball
AREA	30m x 50m channel
AIMS	Support Play, Passing

⬭	Ball
⊗	Player
⌓	Bag
▭	Shield
–·–·–→	Kick/Roll
- - - - →	Run Without a Ball
——→ (blue)	Pass
——→ (red)	Run With a Ball
△	Cone/Marker

Explanation

Players (1-5) static and positioned as above. Begin with player (1) passing to (2), then sprinting to take up position behind and on the outside of (E). The drill continues with all static players passing and racing to take up secondary positions. Player (A) takes the ball from (5) on the run. The ball is passed along the line to (E).
The drill continues with Player (1) taking the next pass on the outside of (E) and transferring to his secondary support as they come through the gaps and so on.

85

SUPPORT PLAY

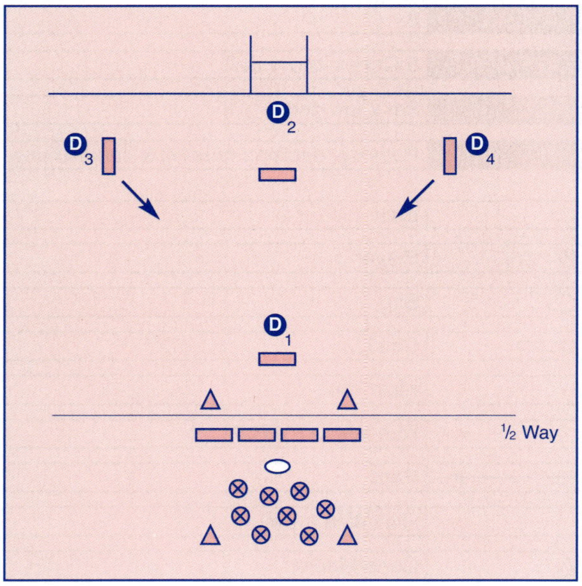

PLAYERS	Two teams of 8
EQUIPMENT	8 Shields, 1 Ball and 10 Cones
AREA	Half a pitch
AIMS	Support Play, Decision Making

⬭	Ball
⊗	Player
⌓	Bag
▭	Shield
–·–·–→	Kick/Roll
- - - - →	Run Without a Ball
——→ (blue)	Pass
——→ (red)	Run With a Ball
△	Cone/Marker

Explanation

The group is split into 2 teams of at least 8 players each. The attacking team is placed in a 15 metre square grid with a ball. They are confronted at the gateway to the grid by 4 defenders carrying shields. The attacking team must combine to beat these shields are leave the grid by the gateway. Once beaten the defenders must retain their position. Once through the grid the attackers are then confronted by defender 1 who is playing as a sweeper. The 8 attackers must beat the sweeping player who again once beaten cannot chase back. Finally the attackers are confronted by a full back (defender 2) who they must combine to beat and score a try, a further progression could be the adding of 2 covering wingers, defenders 3 and 4. Those 2 covering wingers must be conditioned by the coach to only enter play once the shields have been broken.

86

FALL & PASS-ON

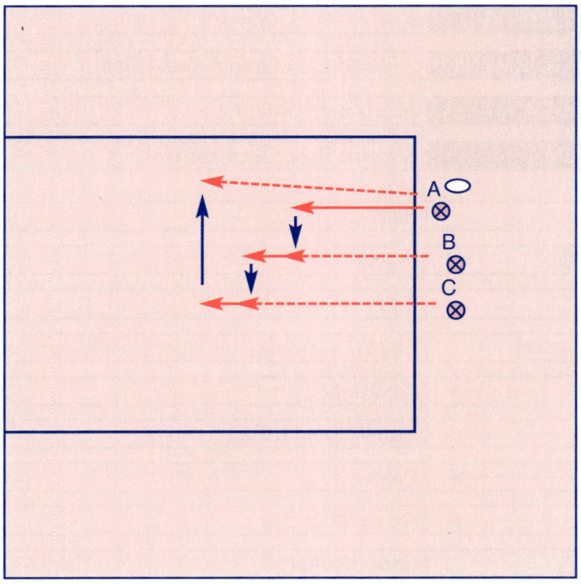

PLAYERS	3
EQUIPMENT	1 Ball
AREA	Over 50m
AIMS	Keep ball alive, support play, up & off the ground fast

	Ball
	Player
	Bag
	Shield
	Kick/Roll
	Run Without a Ball
	Pass
	Run With a Ball
	Cone/Marker

Explanation
Player A with the ball moves forwards. After several steps he falls towards the ground. As he does so he passes the ball inside to player B, B repeats the same procedure and passes as he falls to C. C goes forward falls and passes to A who has regained his feet and supported. The drill continues.

Extension
Larger playing distance.

87

PASS IN THE TACKLE

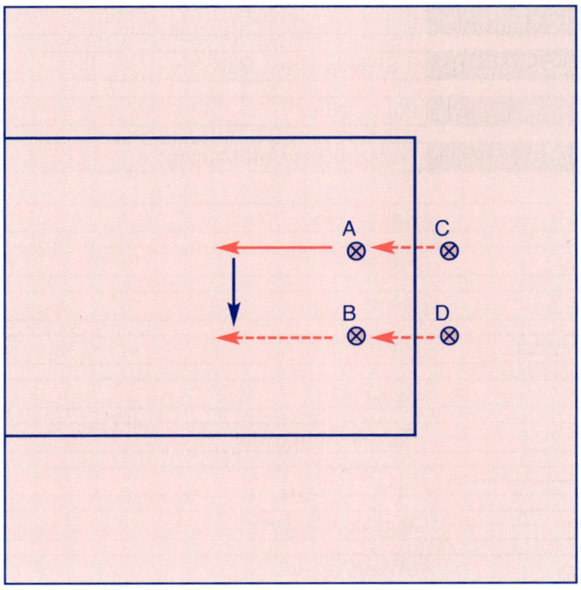

PLAYERS	4
EQUIPMENT	1 Ball
AREA	50 x 60m
AIMS	Support Play, Passing

	Ball
	Player
	Bag
	Shield
	Kick/Roll
	Run Without a Ball
	Pass
	Run With a Ball
	Cone/Marker

Explanation
2 (A&B) attackers with the ball on start line, 2 (C&D) defenders directly behind them, A&B commence jogging & passing. C&D trail as defenders at least 2m back. On the whistle ball carrier sprints forward and one of the defenders tackles from behind. Ball carrier attempts to off load to his partner. The second defender tries to interfere with the pass – NOT tackle the receiver. Players C&D now jog forward and become attackers, A&B become defenders.

88

SUPPORT DRILL 3 V 1

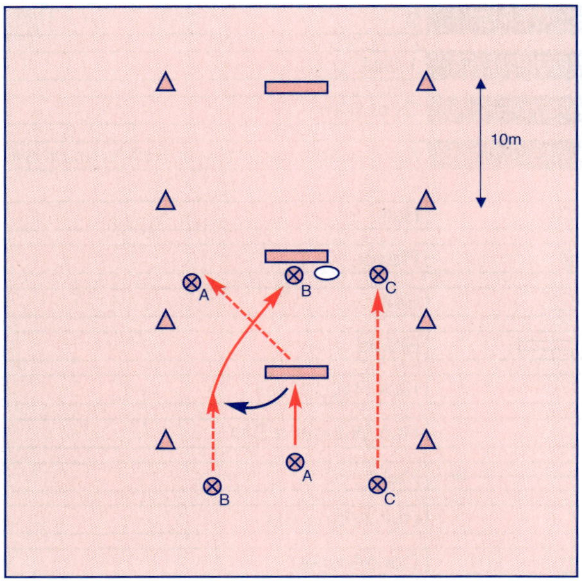

PLAYERS	6
EQUIPMENT	3 Shields, 6 Markers and 1 Ball
AREA	30m x 5m corridor
AIMS	Support Play, Decision Making

⬭	Ball
⊗	Player
◠	Bag
▭	Shield
–·–·–►	Kick/Roll
- - - - ►	Run Without a Ball
——►	Pass
——►	Run With a Ball
△	Cone/Marker

Explanation
3 shields are placed evenly. 3 players with a ball carrier in the middle move down the corridor. The ball carrier draws the shield (who can only move laterally) and lays off a pass. The new ball carrier then attacks the next shield. The man who gave the pass must support the ball carrier in the space which is left. (i.e: in the diagram above (A) has passed to (B). (B) now attacks the next shield and (A) has supported in (B's) original position). The object is to ensure the ball carrier has support left and right.

89

SHIELD DRILL – SUPPORT

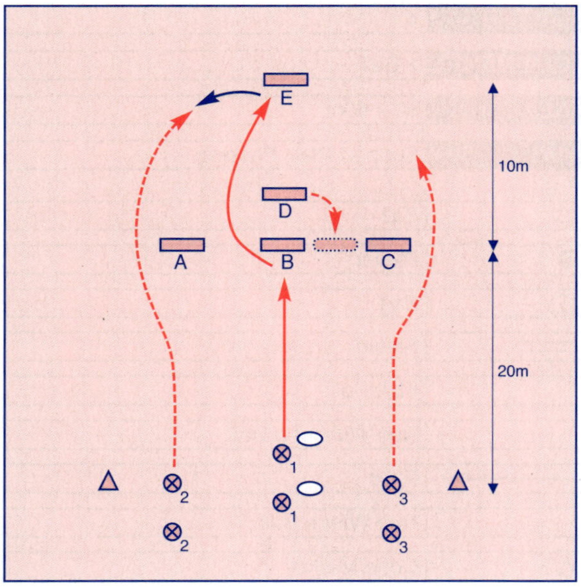

PLAYERS	8
EQUIPMENT	5 Shields and 1 Ball
AREA	20m x 20m
AIMS	Support/Decision Making

⬭	Ball
⊗	Player
◠	Bag
▭	Shield
–·–·–►	Kick/Roll
- - - - ►	Run Without a Ball
——►	Pass
——►	Run With a Ball
△	Cone/Marker

Explanation
Attacker 1 approaches the central point of shields (A), (B) and (C) as he nears them shield (D) fills one of the gaps between the shields causing 1 to sidestep through the available gap. He is then confronted by shield (E).
He hits, spins and off-loads to either 2 and 3 who has supported on the outside.

90

SUPPORT/DECISION MAKING

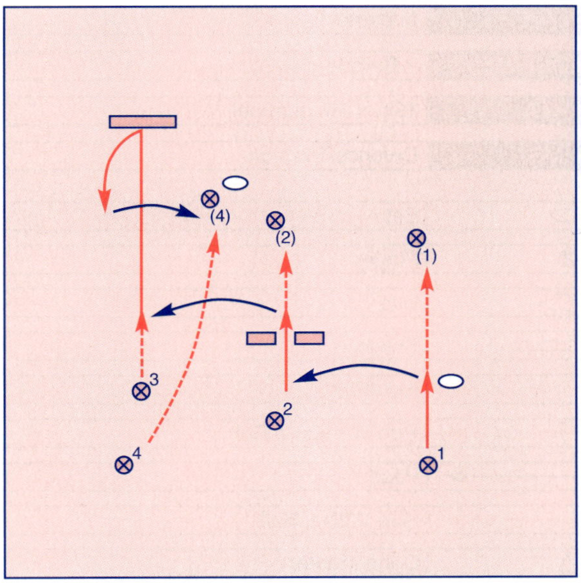

PLAYERS	Unlimited
EQUIPMENT	1 Ball and between 4 and 5 Shields
AREA	25m x 25m
AIMS	Support Play, Decision Making

⬭	Ball
⊗	Player
◠	Bag
▭	Shield
-·-·-·→	Kick/Roll
------→	Run Without a Ball
——→	Pass
——→	Run With a Ball
△	Cone/Marker

Explanation

Player 1 passes to player 2 who attacks and breaks the shields immediately in front of him. On breaking the shields 2 passes to player 3 who hits the shield at B. He hits, spins and off-loads to player 4 who is supporting a short distance behind. Player 4 then has a number of options. A short pass to player 2, a long pass to player 1 or to run across player 2 and execute a drop off. Alternatively player 4 can attack the shield at C and use players 2 and 1 as support.

91

SLIDE DEFENCE

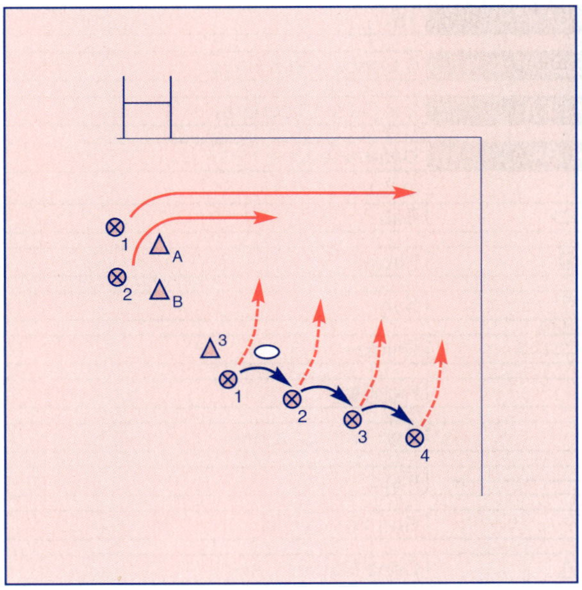

PLAYERS	Groups of 6
EQUIPMENT	3 Cones and 1 Ball
AREA	Quarter of a Pitch
AIMS	Slide Defence, Decisions, Communication

⬭	Ball
⊗	Player
◠	Bag
▭	Shield
-·-·-·→	Kick/Roll
------→	Run Without a Ball
——→	Pass
——→	Run With a Ball
△	Cone/Marker

Explanation

Two defenders are placed by cones (A & B). 4 attackers, with a ball are lined out attacking style across the pitch.
The aim is for the 4 attackers to score a try anywhere between the posts and the corner flag or for the 2 defenders to stop them by executing a 2 handed touch or causing a dropped ball, etc.
As soon as player 1, with the ball, begins to move from markers, the defenders can come into play. This is done by both of the defenders running around markers A and B. The attackers can only move the ball wide, i.e: to the right. No inside balls or drop offs are allowed.
Progression: Introduce a 5th attacker and a 3rd defender who stands as a marker when the ball is played.
The attacking players are allowed one inside (to the left) pass.

92

DEFENCE

PLAYERS	In pairs
EQUIPMENT	2 Balls and 6 Cones
AREA	15m x 5m channel
AIMS	Defence/Evasion

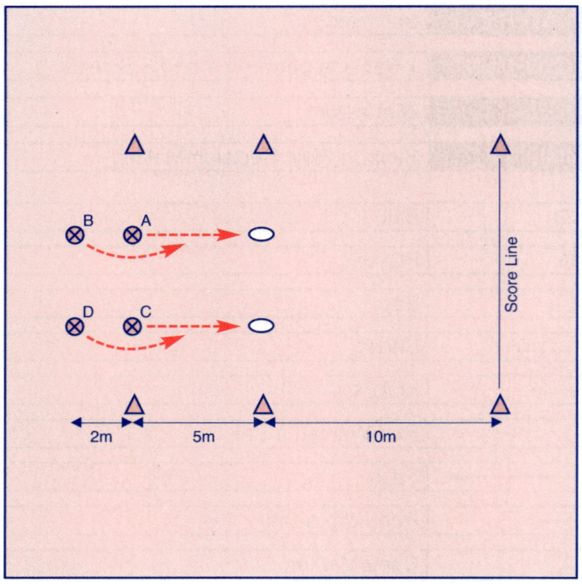

	Ball
	Player
	Bag
	Shield
	Kick/Roll
	Run Without a Ball
	Pass
	Run With a Ball
	Cone/Marker

Explanation
Players pair off in a 15 metre x 5 metre corridor (as per diagram). The first player in each team (A) and (C), sprint out, pick up the ball and attempt to score at the end of the grid. The second players (B) and (D), who start 1 to 3 metres adrift, chase and attempt a two handed tag on the ball carrier before he reaches the score line.
Players reverse roles at the other end.

93

TACKLE BACK RACE

PLAYERS	18
EQUIPMENT	6 Cones and 6 Bags
AREA	2 x (10 x 10 square)
AIMS	Defensive Line

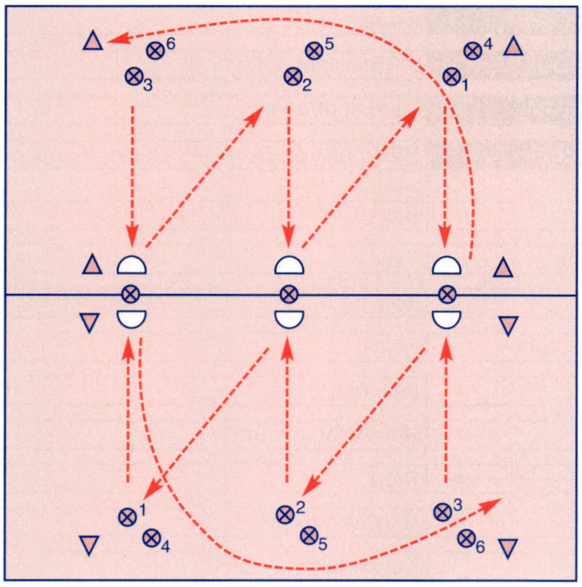

	Ball
	Player
	Bag
	Shield
	Kick/Roll
	Run Without a Ball
	Pass
	Run With a Ball
	Cone/Marker

Explanation
Two squares of the same size are set up as in the diagram, 6 players per square (+ 3 bag holders), X1 X2 & X3 move forward and tackle the bag in front of them. As they retreat X2 & X3 slide to the place on their left (i.e: X2 takes X1 place & X3 takes X2 place), X1 comes back and runs to the right to take X3 place.
When everyone is back in position they immediately move forward and make the 2nd tackle.
On return a similar manoeuvre is repeated after 6 tackles X4, X5, X6, go.

94

1 V 1

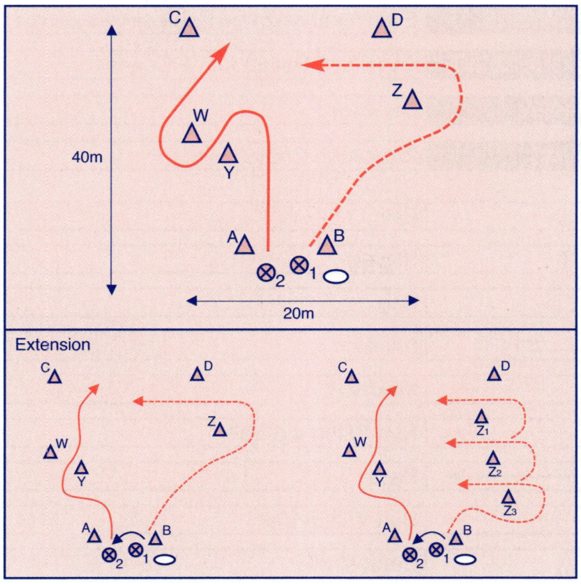

PLAYERS	Groups of 2
EQUIPMENT	7 Cones and 1 Ball between 2
AREA	40m x 20m
AIMS	Evasion – Agility

	Ball
	Player
	Bag
	Shield
	Kick/Roll
	Run Without a Ball
	Pass
	Run With a Ball
	Cone/Marker

Explanation
Players line up in pairs behind cones (A) and (B). Player 1 has the ball. He then passes to player 2 and then runs around cone (2) to attempt a two-handed touch tackle on player 1 who on receiving the ball runs in and out of cones (W) and (Y) and attempts to score between cones (C) and (D).

95

PLAY THE BALL

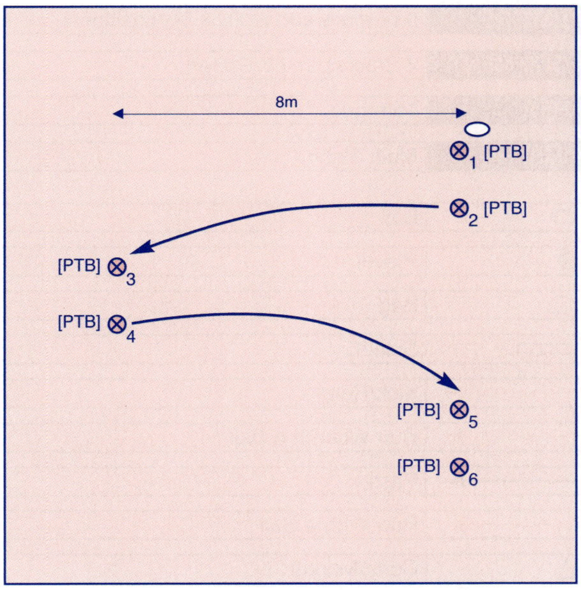

PLAYERS	Minimum 6
EQUIPMENT	3 Markers and 1 Ball
AREA	10m x 10m grid
AIMS	Play the Ball, Pass from the Floor

	Ball
	Player
	Bag
	Shield
	Kick/Roll
	Run Without a Ball
	Pass
	Run With a Ball
	Cone/Marker

Explanation
Split your team into groups of six players, organise as above. The drill begins with player (1) playing the ball to player (2), who passes to (3) (acting half back style). (3) then plays to (4) who passes to (5), who plays the ball to (6). Player (6) sprints to number (1)'s place, whilst all other players adjust accordingly, e.g. (1) moves to (2); (2) moves to (3) and so on, with player (5) ending up in (6)'s original place. The drill continues.

96

DOUBLE MARKER DRILL

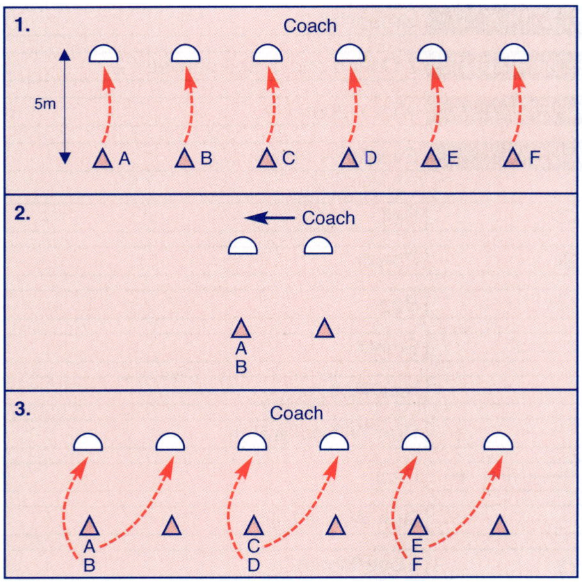

PLAYERS	Even number (2,4,6 or 8 dependant on equipment)
EQUIPMENT	Bags (or Shields) and 6 Cones
AREA	5m x 15m
AIMS	Front Man Chase

	Ball
	Player
	Bag
	Shield
	Kick/Roll
	Run Without a Ball
	Pass
	Run With a Ball
	Cone/Marker

Explanation
Players line up 5m from the bags, with the coach standing behind the bag line. The coach calls "in" and the line attacks the bags. The players are working with partners (i.e: A & B, C & D, E & F). The players retreat in the direction indicated by the coach to form a double marker opposite that bag (see diagram 2).
So looking at A & B – The coach has pointed to the right (A) & (B) have formed up as 1st and 2nd marker in front of A's bag. On the coaches next call of "in" the front marker chases off and takes to spare bag and the 2nd marker holds and then tackles the bag facing him (see diagram 3).
The players then retreat again in the direction indicated by the coach.
Complete 6 tackles and change.

97

PLAY THE BALL ACTIVITY DRILL

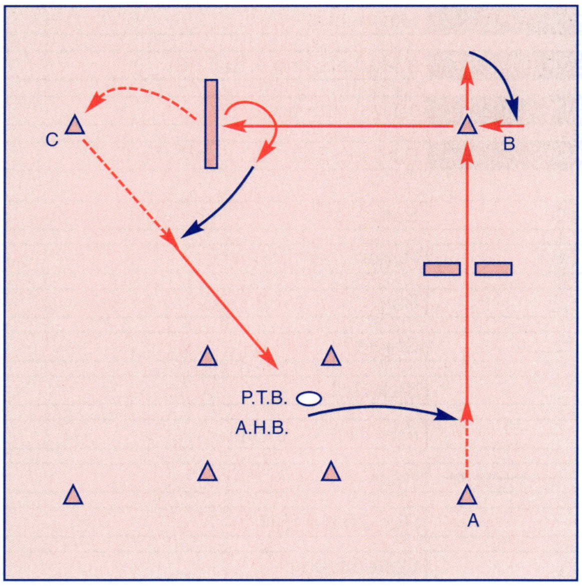

PLAYERS	9 (if more add to R_2 & R_3 positions)
EQUIPMENT	4 Shields and 7 Cones
AREA	15m grid
AIMS	Multi Skills

	Ball
	Player
	Bag
	Shield
	Kick/Roll
	Run Without a Ball
	Pass
	Run With a Ball
	Cone/Marker

Explanation
The ball is played within a 15m grid. The A.H.B. passes to A who busts the shields on his way towards B. A then executes a "drop-off" pass to B who hits and spins to lay off a pass to C on the move.
C makes his way to the P.T.B. area and the drill continues by all players rotating one place (i.e: the player who originally played the ball is now A.H.B. and the A.H.B. becomes A, etc).

NB: Change shield holders periodically.

98

BAG DRILL

1.

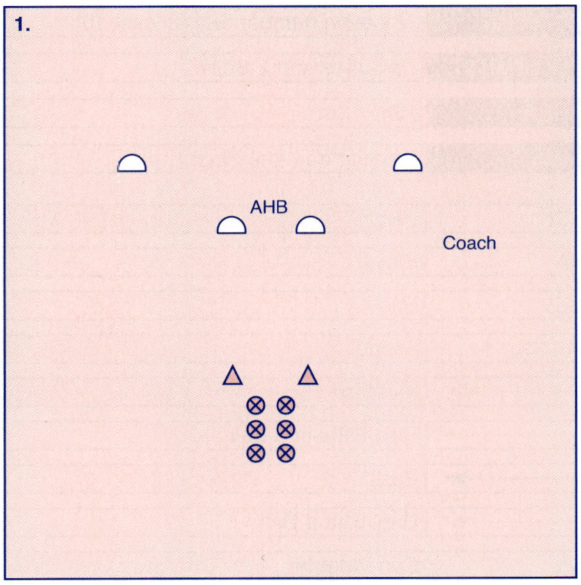

PLAYERS	Minimum 15
EQUIPMENT	8 Cones, 1 Ball, 2 Bags and 2 Shields
AREA	30m x 20m
AIMS	Front marker chase, 2nd marker hold, communication

⬭	Ball
⊗	Player
◠	Bag
▭	Shield
–·–·–·→	Kick/Roll
- - - - →	Run Without a Ball
——→	Pass
——→	Run With a Ball
△	Cone/Marker

Explanation

A player is selected to play AHB. He is placed behind two tackle bags, which are 2m apart. Two more bags are situated at a position on either side of the AHB, where the first receivers would stand (approx. 8m). The rest of the group pair off and stand behind cones 10m away. On a command from the coach the first pair M_1 and M_2 run forward and tackle the two bags immediately in front of them. They regain their feet and adapt a double marker position in front of the AHB (as diagram 2).

The AHB simulates a pass to either of the bags at first receiver. The front marker chases off and tackles the bag which was aimed at by the AHB. The second holds his position momentarily before running to the other side and tackling the other bag (see diagram 3).

The AHB is allowed to dummy and go between the two bags if he/she so wishes. Therefore it is imperative that the second marker (M_2) holds his/her position long enough to cover for that play.

A progression from that drill is to introduce an inside runner in the form of two shields (A) and (B) (see diagram 4). The drill continues in the same manner with the AHB dictating which ways the markers chase. However the coach can now, after the first marker is chasing to tackle a bag, call either shield A or B to set off running in a straight line. It is the second marker's job to pick up this shield who is acting as an inside runner (see diagram 5).

If, for example, the AHB points to his right, the first marker (M_1) chases across and tackles the bag. The coach shouts "A" and shield (A) moves forward. Marker 2 (M_2) holds to check the AHB is not going between the bags and then moves out to tackle shield (A).

2.

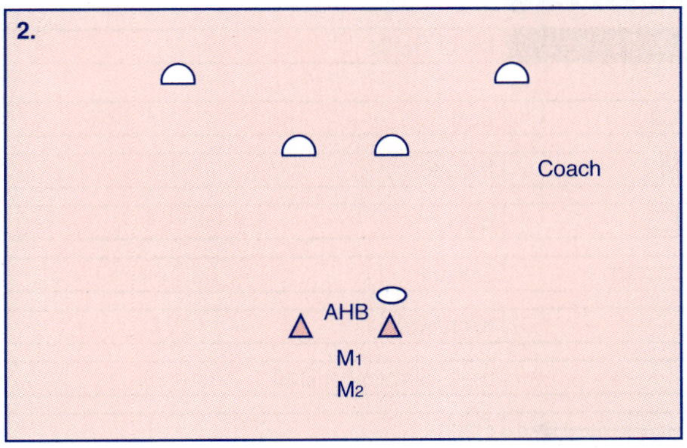

3.

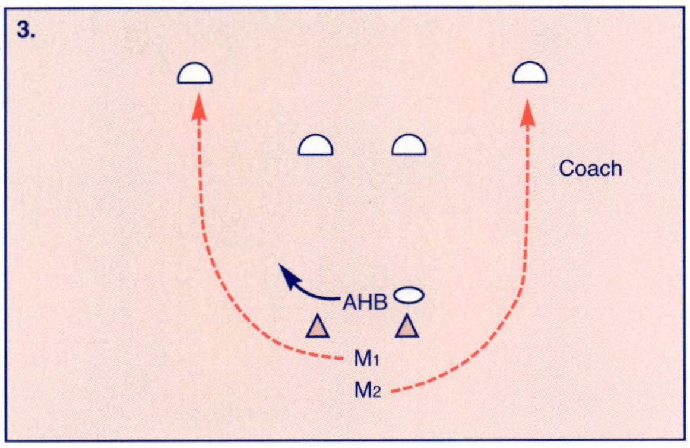

4.

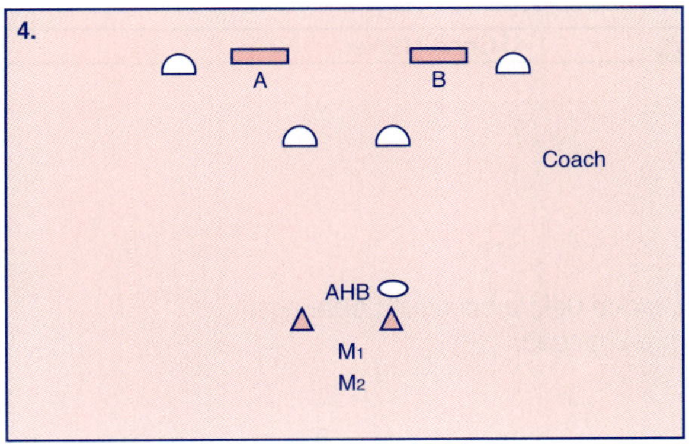

5.

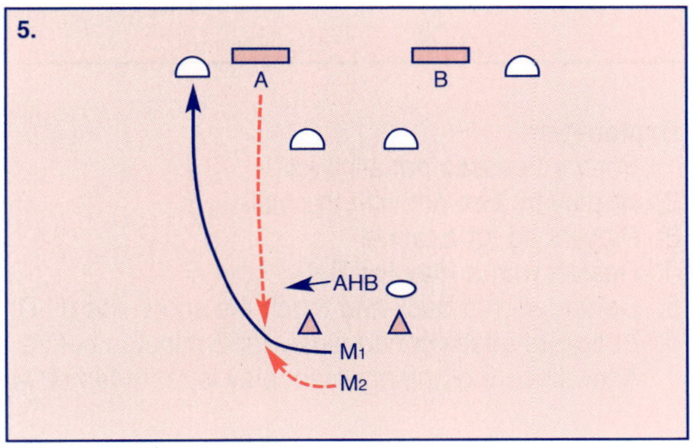

99

ACTING HALF BACK

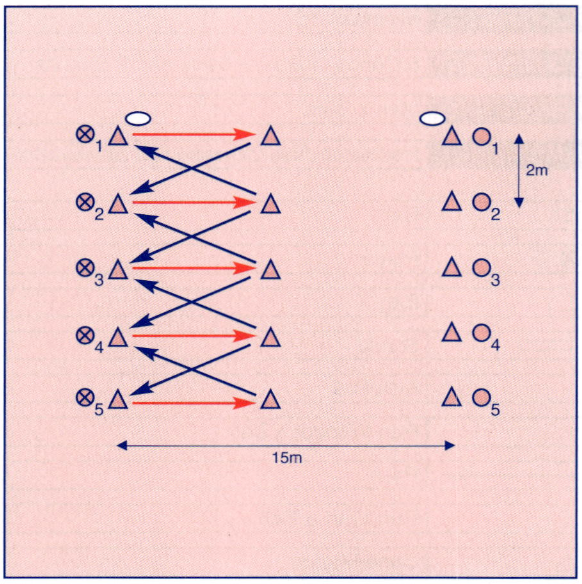

PLAYERS	Any even number (but at least 10)
EQUIPMENT	15 Cones and 2 Balls
AREA	15m x 8m
AIMS	Passing from the Floor

	Ball
	Player
	Bag
	Shield
	Kick/Roll
	Run Without a Ball
	Pass
	Run With a Ball
	Cone/Marker

Explanation
Two teams of 5 players (X & O) are lined up opposite each other 15m apart. On command player 1 runs to the cone in the centre places the ball on the floor and executes an 'acting half back' pass to player 2 who runs onto the centre cone – places the ball on the floor and passes to player 3 and the drill continues until player 5 receives the ball. By having the team opposite do exactly the same a race can develop which places the skills under pressure.

100

GAME

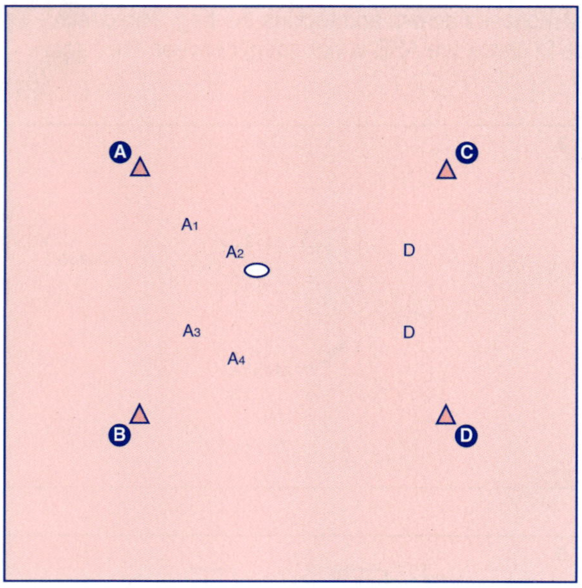

PLAYERS	6
EQUIPMENT	1 Ball and 4 Cones
AREA	20m x 10m grid
AIMS	Multi Skills

	Ball
	Player
	Bag
	Shield
	Kick/Roll
	Run Without a Ball
	Pass
	Run With a Ball
	Cone/Marker

Explanation
1. Forward passes not allowed.
2. All players can run with the ball.
3. Players tig for a tackle.
4. Restart with a Play the Ball.
5. Defenders run back and touch the score-line (C-D) after a tackle before becoming alive again.
6. Attackers attack continuously for 3 minutes before teams are changed.
7. After a score or infringement play is restarted on line A-B.